NEW DIRECTIONS FOR INSTITUTIONAL RESEARCH

# The Effect of Assessment on Minority Student Participation

Michael T. Nettles

*EDITOR*

NUMBER 65, SPRING 1990
JOSSEY-BASS INC., PUBLISHERS

NEW DIRECTIONS FOR INSTITUTIONAL RESEARCH

Patrick T. Terenzini
*The Pennsylvania State University*
*EDITOR-IN-CHIEF*

Ellen Earle Chaffee
*North Dakota Board of Higher Education*
*ASSOCIATE EDITOR*

# The Effect of Assessment on Minority Student Participation

Michael T. Nettles
*University of Tennessee*

*EDITOR*

Number 65, Spring 1990

JOSSEY-BASS INC., PUBLISHERS
San Francisco • Oxford

# aas 7472

The Effect of Assessment on Minority Student Participation. (so# 56640)
*Michael T. Nettles* (ed.).
New Directions for Institutional Research, no. 65.
Volume XVII, Number 1.

NEW DIRECTIONS FOR INSTITUTIONAL RESEARCH
*Patrick T. Terenzini*, Editor-in-Chief
*Ellen Earle Chaffee*, Associate Editor

NEW DIRECTIONS FOR INSTITUTIONAL RESEARCH is part of The
Jossey-Bass Higher Education Series and is published quarterly by
Jossey-Bass Inc., Publishers (publication number USPS 098-830).
Second-class postage paid at San Francisco, California, and at
additional mailing offices. Postmaster: Send address changes to
Jossey-Bass Inc., Publishers, 350 Sansome Street, San Francisco,
California 94104.

EDITORIAL CORRESPONDENCE should be sent to the Editor-in-Chief,
Patrick T. Terenzini, Center for the Study of Higher Education,
133 Willard Building, The Pennsylvania State University,
University Park, Pennsylvania 16802.

august 20, 1990

Library of Congress Catalog Card Number LC 85-645339
International Standard Serial Number ISSN 0271-0579
International Standard Book Number ISBN 1-55542-828-2

Photograph by Chad Slattery, copyright © 1984. All rights reserved.
Manufactured in the United States of America. Printed on acid-free paper.

The Association for Institutional Research was created in 1966 to benefit, assist, and advance research leading to improved understanding, planning, and operation of institutions of higher education. Publication policy is set by its Publications Board.

For information about the Association for Institutional Research, write to:

AIR Executive Office
314 Stone Building
Florida State University
Tallahassee, FL 32306-3038

(904) 644-4470

# CONTENTS

# EDITOR'S NOTES

The student bodies of America's colleges and universities are gradually becoming ethnically diverse. In 1987, 22 percent of the undergraduate students in the United States were nonwhite ethnic minorities, compared with 19 percent in 1977. Of the undergraduate students enrolled in 1987, White students comprised 78 percent, Black students made up 9 percent, 6 percent were Latino, 4 percent were Asian Americans, 1 percent was American Indian; foreign students comprised the remaining 2 percent. Among the minority groups, Blacks were the only group that did not experience an overall enrollment increase between 1977 and 1987. Instead of increasing, Black enrollment declined. The proportion of undergraduate enrollments that Blacks represented declined from 10.2 to 9.2 percent during the period between 1977 and 1986. During the same time, Asian American enrollment increased by 129 percent, Latino enrollment increased by 55 percent, American Indians by 16 percent, and White enrollment by 8 percent (National Center for Educational Statistics, 1977 and 1987; Mow and Nettles, in press).

Increasing the number of minority students and the proportion they represent in the student body, however, is only the first step toward genuine equity of access in American higher education. As the racial and ethnic differences in access and admissions to higher education become narrower, the difference in the performance and experiences of students from diverse ethnic backgrounds appears to be broadening. The lower rates of persistence, performance, satisfaction, and achievement among non-Asian minority students makes assessing college environments, policies, and organization at least as important as, if not more important than, assessing the effects of admissions policies on students upon entry into college.

Assessments of the performance and experiences of students indicate more modest progress toward narrowing the gaps between some minority groups and majority students in certain performance areas. The ratio of females to males attending college is roughly 50:50 for all ethnic groups except Blacks. For Blacks the female-to-male ratio is 62:38 (Lee, 1985; Nettles, 1988c). A higher proportion of American Indians, Blacks, and Latinos who enter college have lower socioeconomic status backgrounds and greater financial need than White and Asian American students (Astin, 1982; Peng, 1985; Olivas, 1986; Nettles, 1987, 1988b, and 1990).

The academic preparation for college among non-Asian minority college students, in general, is inferior to that of their majority and Asian counterparts. While 25 percent of all college freshmen enter college classified as developmental or remedial students, nearly half of Blacks and

Latinos do so (National Center for Educational Statistics, 1986). The college admissions scores of Latinos is roughly 75 points below their White counterparts on each of the mathematical and verbal parts of the Scholastic Aptitude Test (SAT) and the score of Blacks is nearly 100 points below Whites on each part. The Asians who take the SAT score higher than Whites on the mathematical part but lower than Whites on the verbal (Arbeiter, 1986). Black and Latino youth also take fewer math, science, and college-preparatory courses in high school than White and Asian college-bound students, and their high schools are generally of lower quality (Nettles, 1988b). All of these background characteristics are likely to affect changes in the college environment; they also challenge colleges to change some of their practices in order to succeed with minority students.

Among those who enroll in institutions of higher education, American Indians, Asian Americans, Blacks, and Latinos are more likely than their majority counterparts to enter community colleges (National Center for Educational Statistics, 1987; Astin, 1982; and Pelavin, forthcoming) and are more likely to attend public four-year colleges than the large public and private universities that have greater resources (National Center for Educational Statistics, 1987; and Mow and Nettles, in press).

Although colleges and universities are expanding their use of standardized tests to assess student performance, other indicators such as retention in college, progression through the curriculum, grades, and degree completion are also important. Non-Asian minority groups are found to have higher rates of attrition from college, are less likely to receive a degree (Astin, 1982; Hilton and Schrader, 1987), receive lower grades (Goldman and Hewitt, 1976; Mow and Nettles, in press), and progress at a slower pace toward receiving a degree than their Asian and White counterparts (Gosman, Nettles, Dandridge, and Thoeny, 1982; and Lavin, Murtha, Kaufman, and Hyllegard, 1986). Black students, in particular, have also been found to experience social isolation (Peterson and others, 1978; Allen, 1988) and relatively low interaction with faculty (Nettles, 1988a) while attending college. Lack of social and academic integration has been found to be associated with higher attrition and lower performance in college (Tinto, 1975; Pascarella, 1985; Nettles, 1988a).

Finally, what happens to students in terms of graduate school, professional school, and careers is an important assessment issue relative to diversity. Presumably, equal access and success for minority students in undergraduate school should lead to equality in post-baccalaureate opportunities and experiences. Braddock and McPartland (1988) have found that the occupational attainment and earnings of Black students lags behind their White counterparts.

## The Focus of This Book

This issue of New Directions for Institutional Research examines some of the most important assessment issues related to minority access, achievement, performance, and success in higher education and beyond. While a book of this type cannot provide a comprehensive treatment of the issues and topics that need to be addressed in the context of minority participation and achievement in higher education, it introduces and addresses some of the most important topics. These topics are the following:

• Precollegiate preparation for college
• The unique challenges for Asian American minorities
• The effects of new and emerging outcomes-assessment policies upon minority-undergraduate student achievement
• The organization and structural changes needed by the nation's colleges and universities in order to improve performance and experiences of minority students in college
• Minority-student access to graduate school and careers that have rigorous assessment criteria for entry.

In addition to this brief introductory chapter, seven additional chapters are presented.

In Chapter One, Jacqueline Looney presents the results of her survey of the nation's most prestigious graduate institutions and describes the criteria used for admitting students and how some of those criteria serve as obstacles to minority-student access. Looney offers suggestions regarding assessments that can be used by these graduate institutions to increase diversity and minority-student success.

In Chapter Two, Diane J. Simon shows how assessment and testing affect the career access and progress of students while they are enrolled in college and after they graduate. Simon uses the field of teacher education to illustrate how cutoff scores limit minority access to undergraduate teacher-training programs and also prevent a higher proportion of minority college graduates than White college graduates from being certified.

In Chapter Three, Jean J. Endo describes the performance of Asian and Pacific Americans on various performance indicators, including high school grades, college attendance rates, college admissions test scores, college-persistence and graduation rates, and student perceptions about their colleges. Endo's data help clarify some misconceptions about the superiority of all Asian American students, which tend to be based on the performance of Chinese and Japanese students rather than that of other sub-groups.

In Chapter Four, Daryl G. Smith shifts the focus of the assessment issue away from students to assessing institutions and programs. While acknowledging the value of student-centered assessment, Smith argues for balance in the assessment process, whereby institutions assess their programs, activities, and policies in order to identify ways to enhance minority-student acceptance and success.

In Chapter Five, Mildred Garcia describes the implementation of a statewide student outcomes assessment program at Montclair State College. She uses that experience to propose tasks and issues that require careful attention to ensure appropriate treatment of minority students.

In Chapter Six, Roy E. McTarnaghan describes the results and the impact on minorities of Florida's College Academic Skills Test (CLAST). CLAST is a test of basic skills that students in colleges and universities in Florida are required to pass before progressing to their junior year of college.

In Chapter Seven, Janet R. Johnson describes the preparedness of minority high school students for college. Johnson uses the most recent results of the mathematics and science components of the National Assessment of Educational Progress to describe the skills and abilities of the nation's seventeen-year-olds, comparing ethnic minorities with White youth.

In the Conclusion, I highlight the major assessment themes of the prior chapters, summarize the assessment challenges facing minorities in the near future, and present some issues that need to be the target of further research and assessment.

Michael T. Nettles<br>Editor

## References

Allen, W. R. "Improving Black Student Access and Achievement in Higher Education." *Review of Higher Education,* 1988, *11* (4), 403–416.

Arbeiter, S. *Minority Enrollment in Higher Education Institutions: A Chronological View.* New York: College Entrance Examination Board, 1986.

Astin, A. W. *Minorities in American Higher Education: Recent Trends, Current Prospects, and Recommendations.* San Francisco: Jossey-Bass, 1982.

Braddock, F. H., II, and McPartland, J. M. "Some Cost and Benefit Considerations for Black College Students Attending Predominantly White Versus Predominantly Black Universities." In M. T. Nettles (ed.), *Toward Black Undergraduate Student Equality in American Higher Education.* Westport, Conn.: Greenwood Press, 1988.

Goldman, R., and Hewitt, B. "Predicting the Success of Black, Chicano, Oriental, and White College Students." *Journal of Educational Measurement,* 1976, *13* (2), 107–117.

Gosman, E. J., Nettles, M. T., Dandridge, B. A., and Thoeny, A. R. "Student Progression and Attrition in College: Does Race Make a Difference?" Paper presented at the annual meeting of the Association for the Study of Higher Education, Washington, D.C., 1982.

Hilton, T. L., and Schrader, W. B. *Pathways to Graduate School: An Empirical Study Based on National Longitudinal Data.* Princeton, N.J.: Educational Testing Service, 1987.

Lavin, D., Murtha, J., Kaufman, B., and Hyllegard, D. *Long-Term Educational Attainment in an Open-Access University System: Effects of Ethnicity, Economic Status, and College Type*. Paper presented at the annual meeting of the American Educational Research Association, San Francisco, April 1986.

Lee, V. *Access to Higher Education: The Experience of Blacks, Hispanics, and Low Socioeconomic Status Whites*. Washington, D.C.: Division of Policy and Research, American Council on Education, 1985.

Mow, S. L., and Nettles, M. T. "Minority Student Access, Persistence and Performance in Higher Education: A Review of the Trends and Research Literature." In J. C. Smart (ed.), *Higher Education: Handbook of Theory and Research*. Vol. 6. New York: Agathon Press, in press.

National Center for Educational Statistics, Department of Education. *State Higher Education General Information Survey*. Washington, D.C.: U.S. Government Printing Office, 1977, 1986, 1987.

Nettles, M. T. "Precollegiate Development of Minority Scientists and Engineers." In L. S. Dix (ed.), *Minorities: Their Underrepresentation and Career Differentials in Science and Engineering*. Washington, D.C.: National Academy Press, 1987.

Nettles, M. T. "Factors Related to Black and White Students' College Performance." In M. T. Nettles (ed.), *Toward Black Undergraduate Student Equality in American Higher Education*. Westport, Conn.: Greenwood Press, 1988a.

Nettles, M. T. "Introduction: Contemporary Barriers to Black Student Equality in Higher Education." In M. T. Nettles (ed.), *Toward Black Undergraduate Student Equality in American Higher Education*. Westport, Conn.: Greenwood Press, 1988b.

Nettles, M. T. (ed.). *Toward Black Undergraduate Student Equality in American Higher Education*. Westport, Conn.: Greenwood Press, 1988c.

Nettles, M. T. *Black, Hispanic, and White Doctoral Students: Before, During, and After Enrolling in Graduate School*. Princeton, N.J.: Graduate Record Examination Board and Educational Testing Service, 1990.

Nettles, M. T., Gosman, E. J., Thoeny, A. R., and Dandridge, B. A. *Causes and Consequences of College Students Performance—A Focus on Black and White Students' Attrition Rates, Profession, and Grade Point Average*. Nashville: Tennessee Higher Education Commission, 1985.

Olivas, M. A. "Financial Aid for Hispanics: Access, Ideology, and Packaging Policies." In M. A. Olivas (ed.), *Latino College Students*. New York: Teachers College Press, 1986.

Pascarella, E. T. "College Environmental Influence on Learning and Cognitive Development: A Critical Review and Synthesis." In J. C. Smart (ed.), *Higher Education: Handbook of Theory and Research*. Vol. 1. New York: Agathon Press, 1985a.

Pascarella, E. T. "Racial Differences in the Factors Influencing Bachelor's Degree Completion: A Nine-Year Follow-Up." *Research in Higher Education*, 1985b, *23* (4), 351–373.

Pelavin, S. H., Kane, M. B., and Levine, A. B. *Minority Participation in Higher Education*. Forthcoming.

Peng, S. S. "Enrollment Pattern of Asian American Students in Postsecondary Education." Paper presented at the annual meeting of the American Educational Research Association, Chicago, 1985.

Peterson, M. W., Blackburn, R. T., Gamson, Z. F., Arce, C. H., Davenport, R. W., and Mingle, J. R. *Black Students on White Campuses: The Impact of Increased Black Enrollments*. Ann Arbor: Institute for Social Research, University of Michigan, 1978.

Tinto, V. "Dropout from Higher Education: A Theoretical Synthesis of Recent Research." *Educational Research*, 1975, *45*, 89–125.

*Michael T. Nettles is vice-president for assessment at the University of Tennessee.*

*We cannot continue to define academic quality using standards set from a limited perspective and expect students from diverse backgrounds and cultures to meet them. We must consider the wide variety of circumstances that influence their lives.*

# Assessing Minorities for Graduate Admissions

*Jacqueline Looney*

In 1976, the National Board on Graduate Education (NBGE) prepared a special report under a mandate from the Conference Board of Associated Research Councils on *Minority Group Participation in Graduate Education.* The report concluded that very few U.S. minorities (Blacks, Chicanos, Puerto Ricans, and American Indians) held advanced degrees and that equality of access for minorities to graduate education in the United States had yet to become a reality. Today, the issue of minority participation in graduate education remains a key point on the American higher-education agenda (Chandler, 1988; Wilson and Melendez, 1986; Wilson and Carter, 1988).

Although significant progress for minorities was evident in the late 1960s and early 1970s, it is notable that at the time of the 1976 report, minority participation had already peaked. Now, at each level of educational attainment, Blacks, Latinos, and American Indians consistently lose ground when compared with their White and Asian counterparts (Astin, 1982; *Equality and Excellence: The Educational Status of Black Americans,* 1985; *One-Third of a Nation,* 1988).

Researchers have found that minority students are often denied access to graduate degree programs because they do not meet established admissions criteria (Katz and Hartnett, 1976; Office of Civil Rights and U.S. Department of Education, 1984). The Office of Civil Rights (1984) reported that the decentralized admissions process employed by most graduate schools results in inconsistent assessment of applicants for graduate study. Thus, many educators are concerned that as minority students attempt to enter graduate degree programs, they may encounter subtle

New Directions for Institutional Research, no. 65, Spring 1990 © Jossey-Bass Inc., Publishers

forms of discrimination. Pruitt and Isaac (1985) suggest that "a university must look for sources of discrimination in traditional procedures and must invest time and money in redesigning those procedures" (p. 527).

Historically, selective admissions criteria such as test scores were not used for admission into graduate programs. Students were admitted, in many instances, on the basis of their social status and background (Cook, 1970; Gardner, 1984; Sanford, 1976; Weschler, 1984). Selective admissions based on test scores originated after World War II when Jews and members of other minority groups began to demand access (Weschler, 1984).

Although the long-term predictive validity of standardized test scores is uncertain, such scores are still heavily used in admissions practices. To date, a student's score on the Graduate Record Examination (GRE) seems only to predict the student's performance during the first year of graduate school *(Guide to the Use of the Graduate Record Examinations Program,* 1989-1990; Wilson, 1979). In a 1985 study, Scott and Shaw compared the relationship between the GRE scores and performance of Black and White students. Their findings showed that as White students' GRE scores increased their GPAs, or grade-point averages increased, but that as Black students' GRE scores increased their GPAs decreased. The researchers cited the poor predictive ability of the GRE as one of the reasons for this discrepancy.

Concerning minority students, the GRE Guide (1989-1990) states: "GRE scores, like those on similar standardized tests, cannot completely represent the potential of any person, nor can they alone reflect an individual's chances of long-term success in an academic environment. GRE tests provide measures of certain types of developed abilities and achievement, reflecting educational and cultural experience over a long period. Special care is required in interpreting the GRE scores of students who may have had an educational and cultural experience somewhat different from that of the traditional majority" (p. 14).

Since the inception of standardized tests to assess applicants for graduate study, graduate admissions personnel have been advised to use test scores with much caution and as only one of several criteria in predicting a student's academic success; for instance, a 1925 College Board report cited by Pruitt and Isaac (1985) made the cogent point that ". . . test scores are more certain indices of ability than disability. A high score in the test is significant. A low score may or may not be significant" (p. 530). Attitudes, values, motivation, determination, and creativity may play an equally important role in assessing an individual's potential for success academically or otherwise. Unfortunately, attempts to measure these characteristics are not systematic and are not normally used in the admissions process.

Minority access to graduate education has been the subject of much debate but little research (Duncan, 1976; Katz and Hartnett, 1976; Malaney, 1987). A review of the literature on graduate education by Malaney revealed that one of the most popular areas of research has been matriculation, which includes admissions, but very little of this research has focused on minorities.

With the changes now occurring in the demographics of the United States and the economic implications of these trends, it has become increasingly important to examine minority students' access to high-quality education with the goal of achieving greater minority-student enrollment (*Equality and Excellence,* 1985; *One-Third of a Nation,* 1988). This chapter examines how admissions criteria are used, and the impact these criteria have on minority-student access. This chapter has two goals: first, to present the graduate-admissions process of ten selective universities; and second, to present the perceptions of fifty currently enrolled graduate students regarding various admissions factors.

## The Graduate-Admissions Process at Selective Universities

Graduate-school administrators at ten selective private universities in the United States were interviewed about their graduate-admissions process and the effect of this process on minority-student admissions. These universities were selected because of their common prestige and concern about increasing minority enrollment.

The interview questions fall into four categories: (1) admissions criteria; (2) the effect of these criteria on minorities; (3) minority presence in the schools; and (4) minority initiatives. The names of all participating schools have been kept confidential.

*Admissions Criteria.* The criteria commonly used and considered most crucial for admission into the schools interviewed are the undergraduate grade-point average (GPA), Graduate Record Examination (GRE) scores, the quality of the student's undergraduate school, recommendations, and a personal statement by the student. A few of the schools indicated that while there was no general requirement for the GRE, individual departments may require it as well as other criteria, such as writing samples and personal interviews. In fact, some departments might rely heavily on the GRE for their admission decisions.

For the majority of the schools, the departments recommend admissions decisions to the graduate dean. In most cases, but not all, the graduate school has the formal authority to admit or overturn an admissions recommendation; the latter rarely occurs. Sometimes, the graduate dean requests additional information on applicants, and departments are asked to review the applicant's credentials again. In several schools, admissions guidelines are established solely by the department.

Only three of the ten administrators interviewed had specified minimum undergraduate GPAs and GRE scores. Although most administrators reported no specific cutoff scores for these two criteria (except for the TOEFL for foreign applicants), one stated that "it is pretty much expected that low GREs and GPAs keep you out of the running." Some administrators emphasized that the weight given to the criteria vary by department, with some implied but unwritten minimum standards.

The size of departmental admissions committees varies, with little or no student involvement, although students are involved in the departmental and graduate-school recruitment activities. The majority of the administrators reported small minority-faculty presence on the committees.

*Impact of Criteria on Minorities.* Surprisingly, eight of the ten graduate schools did not keep records on how well minorities fared on their admissions criteria. Five of the schools had some unquantified observations to make, whereas only two were able to share data. Perceptions were, generally, that Whites out-performed Blacks and Latinos, while Asians scored as well or better than Whites on most criteria. The American Indian population was too small to get a sense of their performance. However, one participant indicated that most minority students met its established criteria for admission.

One of the administrators summarized the attitude toward collecting and reporting this kind of information, saying, "Each person is evaluated on an individual basis. We do not keep this information in our data base. We do not use the GRE alone to reject or admit an applicant." Other representatives were concerned that establishing a data base of GRE scores would increase the tendency of departments to focus on the GRE as the main criterion for admission.

None of the schools surveyed used alternative criteria in assessing minority applicants. For one school, the application form provided options for identifying race and gender, but the majority of applicants did not provide this information; consequently, the school had no way of identifying their graduate school applicants in these ways. The majority of the schools encouraged their departments to use flexibility in the use of admissions criteria, while still maintaining admission standards. One representative said, "We encourage flexibility with the GRE; at the same time, scores are still used when we talk about quality." To bring admissible minorities with weak areas "up to speed," one school makes provisions which might include special courses, while another stresses the importance of looking for strengths or signs of admissibility instead of signs to reject, which is the usual procedure. In addition, some schools have developed ways to monitor the assessment of minority applicants: Minority applications are read in the department and then by someone outside the department. One program, in particular, assigns an associate or assistant dean the responsibility of overseeing the minority admissions for each academic division. The specific goal is to look at minority applicants who have been rejected and try to gather more information on the students. According to the representative, "departments are receptive and expect this process to occur." This same school makes six to eight affirmative-action offers to students who might not ordinarily have been admitted but are clearly admissible. A second school has an assistant dean designated to monitor all incoming minority applications; departments are then notified about applicants that look promising before the application is complete. In a third school, departments are asked to review the application differently by focusing on the criteria in the following order: (1) recommendations, (2) statement of purpose, (3) transcripts, and (4) GRE scores and GPA. The idea is to read the application with the aim of understanding the student's background, thus broadening the perception of the student's capabilities. Although a number of the schools make such efforts as these, some are concerned that they do not have the staff to give sufficient attention to minority-applicant files.

Departments vary but appear to be generally flexible in assessing minority applicants. Realistically, as one participant stated, "you [in central administration] don't know what takes place in the department." At one school, some departments designated advocates for female applicants and Black applicants. In another school's social-sciences program, if it is clear that admissible Ph.D. candidates have a number of weaknesses, they are offered admission in a master's program; after successfully completing their master's, they are then recommended for admission into the Ph.D. program. These students are guaranteed funding during and after their qualifying year in the master's program.

While none of the schools actually favored alternative criteria, the majority encouraged their departments to be flexible in assessing applicants. Only one respondent expressed a completely negative attitude toward the use of alternative criteria for minorities: "the University is against special criteria." Still another respondent felt confident that minority applicants were reviewed fairly because their race was not identified on the application. Two predominant attitudes prevailed: First, every effort has to be made to encourage minority students to do well throughout their undergraduate academic career so that they will qualify for admissions into graduate school; and, second, minority applicants must be assessed with an understanding of their backgrounds. There is a general sense among the respondents that a number of the schools have a strong affirmative-action process, as indicated by one representative: "What very often happens is that for minority students, the personal statement becomes much more important. It is not always the aptitude with the [GRE] scores [that decides admissibility]." In many instances, the personal statement provides more insight into a student's background and training than other criteria.

Unfortunately, none of the graduate schools had conducted validity studies to examine the relationship between students' background and preparation (GRE, GPA) and their performance in, retention of the material of, and completion of a graduate program. Some departments conducted validity studies periodically, but not with enough frequency to obtain substantial data on their minority or nonminority students.

*Minority Presence.* The graduate schools surveyed are by design small and intend to remain small. The average student population of the graduate schools surveyed is 1,764, excluding the students enrolled in professional programs. Five of the schools provided data on their 1988–1989 enrollments, but only four were able to give gender and race breakdowns. These limited data suggest that Asian males and Black females comprise the largest percentage, with 26 percent and 20 percent, respectively, of the total minorities in these graduate schools.

It was even more difficult to obtain a profile of minority applications, admissions, and matriculations for 1988–1989. Only three of the ten schools provided complete data; these data suggested that Asian students consistently represented the largest number of applications, admissions, and matriculations, followed by Blacks. The difference in the number of applications made by Latinos and Blacks was minimal; however, Blacks fared better than Latinos in admissions and matriculations. American Indians were virtually nonexistent throughout the whole process.

Seven schools provided information on the gender and racial makeup of the arts-and-sciences faculty, but such information was unavailable for most schools. Because of policy regulations, two of the schools were not at liberty to divulge information on faculty size or makeup. The available information indicates that the average size of the arts-and-sciences faculty is 636, with few minorities but growing numbers of female faculty. A large number of the representatives stated that the numbers of minority faculty were small but growing. New recruitment activities seem to give evidence of a persistent effort to increase minority participation.

*Minority Initiatives.* Many of the schools have launched special initiatives to increase minority enrollment. These initiatives range from using the GRE Locater Service to identify potential minority applicants from those taking the Graduate Record Examination, to establishing named university fellowships for minorities, to developing full-fledged graduate-recruitment programs for minorities and university divisions of minority affairs.

The interviews revealed three categories of recruitment activities. Four to seven of the schools engaged in school visits and recruiting fairs or summer research programs, used the GRE Locater Service or national name exchanges, provided university fellowships for minorities, joined recruitment consortia, or produced special publications, or performed all of these. Three schools were gradually developing student-involvement activities that included graduate-student support groups, graduate-education workshops for their own undergraduates, programs to recruit from regional colleges, and outreach programs with predominantly minority high schools. One to two of the schools had begun novel efforts that are engaging the growing interest of many. These efforts include hosting weekends for newly-admitted minority graduate students, opening student slots specifically for affirmative-action admissions, establishing graduate-recruitment offices, and creating university divisions of minority affairs at the senior administrative and tenured faculty levels. These activities represent some of the more visible forms of university-wide commitment to minority education and therefore warrant some discussion.

Minority-student weekends are not alternatives to the more common visits made by individual prospective students, but rather represent, as stated by one interviewee, "another effort to get the students to accept offers of admissions." Visiting as a group provides psychological support to students and gives them the opportunity to meet other potential graduate-school colleagues. Students invited to participate in such weekends are provided free lodging, usually with enrolled students and faculty, transportation, and meals.

Affirmative-action slots are school-admission slots set aside for minority students "who are admissible" but who might have had difficulty meeting the criteria of a particular department, according to one representative university. Moreover, affirmative-action admissions are fully funded at this university. This affirmative-action plan is not the only route through which minorities enter this graduate program, but it provides assurance of minority-student participation in the program each year. The school's affirmative-action admissions program has been in place since the 1960s.

While most of the schools interviewed have an established core of effective recruitment strategies, only one school has under the aegis of the graduate dean an office whose specific function is coordinating graduate recruitment activities. The assistant dean in this office works closely with faculty in all departments in an effort to expand departmental recruiting efforts, to establish linkages with colleges and professional associations, to seek external funding for support of graduate fellowships, to provide general counseling support for students, and to bring the larger resources of the university to bear on the issue of increasing minority participation in higher education.

Some schools across the country have begun to establish university-level divisions of minority affairs (Green, 1989). According to Green, "Some of those officials serve as directors of minority cultural centers, while others are appointed dean, or vice-president, or in at least one instance, vice-provost for minority affairs" (p. A32). Of the universities surveyed, one has an assistant provost of minority affairs, while another has initiated a nationwide search for a vice-president to direct and administer programs to enhance racial and ethnic diversity at all levels of its university. Positions of this nature should be closely monitored so that the onus is not on this one individual to solve a university's racial problems (Green, 1989). These initiatives go further than verbal commitments and approach the heart of the minority-participation issue.

While funding the higher education of minorities is not new, it remains a primary and common strategy used by schools to attract students. For many of the schools that participated, the strategy is successful and continues to be developed. According to one participant, "Any minority student admitted is given aid. The need issue doesn't usually come into play." To be sure, this was not the prevailing attitude of all the schools surveyed. As one participant stated, "We don't fund anyone very well. Only one-third of the entering class will receive fellowship aid." Some schools have done better than others with the minority-funding issue. In all of the participating schools, all fellowship awards are based on academic merit. Minority applicants also compete for other available fellowships and are not limited to minority fellowship support. Two of the schools did not have minority fellowships; as a representative explained, "All fellowships are merit-based. No special funds are designated for minorities." Another school participant stated that "All students admitted are fully supported; therefore, there is no need to have special support. We try to encourage minorities—being basically in the sciences, we don't see many minorities."

While there are some encouraging developments in the graduate-admissions process overall, very few real changes have been made. Traditional criteria for admissions still dominate the academy. Despite the lack of cutoff scores, students' performance on quantitative indices (their GRE scores and GPAs) remains the basis for admissions decisions, thereby defining quality applicants in a very narrow sense. Alternative criteria are not considered, but flexibility in reviewing minority applicants is encouraged. Only a small number of schools monitor admissions decisions, particularly in regard to minorities. Moreover, the minority presence in many departments is small, which gives very little, if any, minority faculty perspective on the admissions process.

Additionally, data bases are not set up to monitor minority-student performance. Sadly, most schools assume that their minority students follow the national trends in academic achievement and thus do not develop the means to keep track of their actual academic performance.

This dearth of information hampers graduate and university administrators because they cannot adequately identify their minority populations. Only a small number of schools have the staff and commitment to properly monitor minority admissions decisions, a deficiency that is compounded by a lack of resources to establish a core of substantive recruiting activities, by departments' adherence to different sets of standards, and by lack of follow-up on student performance. This results in a reliance on national trends to set the tone and attitude of those who assess minority applicants. As we usher in the twenty-first century, it is abundantly clear that much more work must be done to develop a broader definition of academic quality and that new methods must be formulated to provide proper assessment of minority graduate-school applicants and students.

## Graduate-Student Perceptions of Admissions Factors

While students have few problems obtaining information about application procedures and admissions requirements, graduate schools have not done an adequate job of educating students about the admissions process (Hartnett, 1979; Powers and Lehman, 1983). Accordingly, students do not have a keen sense of how universities evaluate their applications. It is clear from the schools interviewed that departments have autonomy in selecting their admissions criteria and establishing their own departmental admissions process. Moreover, graduate-school administrators often lack knowledge of the admissions process within individual departments. In spite of the difficulty of obtaining information on the admissions process, Hartnett (1979) contends that applicants assign different degrees of importance to the criteria, which may affect their decision where to apply and how to present themselves for consideration.

Interestingly, Powers and Lehman (1983) found that GRE candidates believed that the undergraduate grade-point average (GPA) was the most important factor in admission, followed by recommendations and the undergraduate field. They believed that GRE scores were less important. However, the authors found that Black candidates perceived GRE scores to be significantly more important than White candidates.

To test the latter finding, fifty currently-enrolled, randomly-selected graduate students (17 Black, 25 White, 4 Latino, and 4 Asian) were asked to give their perceptions of the graduate-admissions factors identified by Powers and Lehman (1983) and Powers and Swinton (1982). The subjects were asked to rate the factors in the question that follows on a 4-point scale using the following values: 1 = Hardly any or none, 2 = A little, 3 = Some, 4 = A lot.

How much emphasis do you think your graduate department places on each of the following factors in determining admissions?

A. GRE Aptitude Test verbal score
B. GRE Aptitude Test quantitative score
C. GRE Aptitude Test analytical score
D. GRE Advanced Test score
E. Undergraduate grades
F. Undergraduate major field
G. Academic reputation of undergraduate college
H. Recommendations.

Recommendations were perceived as the most important factor, followed by the undergraduate GPA and the undergraduate major field, while GRE test scores were rated the least important. Aside from the fact that the undergraduate GPA and recommendations appeared in reverse order in the Powers and Lehman (1983) study, the results were identical.

As shown in Table 1, with the exception of the GRE advanced test scores, when Black- and White-student perceptions were compared, Blacks rated GRE scores significantly higher than did Whites, thus confirming Powers and Lehman's findings. This finding is significant: Black and White students are receiving different messages on the importance of the GRE scores. Black students are aware of the history of non-Asian minorities scoring consistently low and are more inclined to expect to perform poorly. As a result, Black students are perhaps more uncomfortable with tests.

Powers and Lehman (1983) suggest that "Black candidates may rate test scores as more important because they see them as being more instrumental in determining their chances for admission." The perception of Black candidates appears to be true, despite any disclaimers that the GRE is not a prevalent factor in the admissions process (Hartnett and Feldmesser, 1980; Baird, 1982). Black students have a more realistic perception of the importance of such test scores in determining their entrance into graduate programs.

The use of standardized tests will continue in the academy. Therefore, it is incumbent on university and college systems to gain a more complete understanding of what actually occurs in their admissions processes and to inform minority students on what determines access to graduate programs. At the same time, undergraduate colleges will have to develop better ways to prepare their students, particularly minority students, for graduate-admissions tests. Most importantly, we cannot continue to define academic quality using standards set from a limited perspective and expect students from diverse backgrounds and cultures to meet them. We must take into consideration the wide variety of circumstances that influence their lives.

**Table 1. Ratings of Student Perceptions of GRE Factors**

| GRE Factors | Black Rating | White Rating |
|---|---|---|
| A. Verbal score | 2.58 | 2.28 |
| B. Quantitative score | 2.75 | 2.08 |
| C. Analytical score | 2.62 | 2.16 |
| D. Advanced Test score | 2.14 | 2.13 |

# References

Astin, A. W. *Minorities in American Higher Education: Recent Trends, Current Prospects, and Recommendations.* San Francisco: Jossey-Bass, 1982.

Baird, L. L. *An Examination of the Graduate Study Application and Enrollment Decisions of GRE Candidates.* Preliminary final report (GRE No. 79-11). Princeton, N.J.: Educational Testing Service, February 1982.

Chandler, T. L. *Enhancing the Minority Presence in Graduate Education.* Washington, D.C.: CGS Idea Exchange, Council of Graduate Schools, 1988.

College Entrance Examination Board. *Equality and Excellence: The Educational Status of Black Americans.* New York: College Entrance Examination Board, 1985.

Cook, W. D. "Recruiting Black Graduate Students." Paper presented at the Conference on the Recruiting of Black Graduate Students, Cornell University, Ithaca, N.Y., 1970.

Duncan, B. L. "Minority Students." In J. Katz and R. T. Hartnett (eds.), *Scholars in the Making.* Cambridge, Mass.: Ballinger, 1976.

Educational Testing Service. *Guide to the Use of the Graduate Record Examinations Program.* Princeton, N.J.: Graduate Record Examinations Board, 1988-89.

Gardner, J. W. *Excellence: Can We Be Equal and Excellent Too?* New York: Norton, 1984.

Green, E. "Minority Affairs Officials, Picked to Help Campuses Improve Racial Climate, Report Some Progress." *Chronicle of Higher Education,* March 22, 1989, pp. A32-A34.

Hartnett, R. T. "The Information Needs of Prospective Graduate Students" (GRE Board Report, GREB No. 77-8R). Princeton, N.J.: Educational Testing Service, 1979.

Hartnett, R. T., and Feldmesser, R. A. "College Admissions Testing and the Myth of Selectivity: Unresolved Questions and Needed Research." *American Association for Higher Education Bulletin,* March 1980.

Katz, J., and Hartnett, R. T. "Recommendations for Training Better Scholars." In J. Katz and R. T. Hartnett (eds.), *Scholars in the Making.* Cambridge, Mass.: Ballinger, 1976.

Malaney, G. D. "A Decade of Research on Graduate Students: A Review of the Literature in Academic Journals." Paper presented at the meeting of the Association for the Study of Higher Education, Baltimore, Md., November 21-24, 1987.

National Board of Graduate Education. *Minority Group Participation in Graduate Education.* Washington, D.C.: National Academy of Sciences, 1976.

Office of Civil Rights and U.S. Department of Education. *Minority Enrollment in Graduate and Professional Schools: Technical Assistance Handbook.* New York: Boone, Young and Associates, 1984.

*One-Third of a Nation: A Report of the Commission on Minority Participation in American Life.* Washington, D.C.: American Council on Education and Education Commission of the States, 1988.

Powers, D. E., and Lehman, J. "GRE Candidates' Perceptions of the Importance of Graduate Admissions Factors." *Research in Higher Education,* 1983, *19* (2), 231-249.

Powers, D. E., and Swinton, S. S. *The Effects of Self-Study of Test Familiarization Materials for the Analytical Section of the GRE Aptitude Test* (GRE Board Report, GREB No. 79-9). Princeton, N.J.: Educational Testing Service, 1982.

Pruitt, A. S., and Isaac, P. D. "Discrimination in Recruitment, Admission, and Retention of Minority Graduate Students." *Journal of Negro Education*, 1985, *54* (4), 526–536.

Sanford, N. "Graduate Education, Then and Now." In J. Katz and R. T. Hartnett (eds.), *Scholars in the Making*. Cambridge, Mass.: Ballinger, 1976.

Scott, R. R., and Shaw, M. E. "Black and White Performance in Graduate School and Policy Implications of the Use of Graduate Record Examinations Scores in Admissions." *Journal of Negro Education*, 1985, *54* (1), 14–23.

Weschler, H. S. "The Rationale for Restriction: Ethnicity and College Admission in America, 1910–1980." *American Quarterly*, 1984, *36* (5), 643–667.

Wilson, K. M. *The Validation of GRE Scores as Predictors of First-Year Performance in Graduate Study: Report of the GRE Cooperative Validity Studies Project*. Princeton, N.J.: Educational Testing Service, 1979.

Wilson, R., and Carter, D. J. *Minorities in Higher Education, Seventh Annual Status Report*. Washington, D.C.: American Council on Education, 1988.

Wilson, R., and Melendez, S. E. *Minorities in Higher Education, Fifth Annual Status Report*. Washington, D.C.: American Council on Education, 1986.

*Jacqueline Looney is assistant dean for graduate recruitment at Duke University.*

*Teacher screening examinations lack content validity and*
*eliminate high proportions of potential minority teachers.*

# The Impact of Assessment Policies on Minority Achievement and Participation in Teacher Education

*Diane J. Simon*

The 1980s was a decade in which numerous national education reform reports stressed the need to achieve excellence in American education. The highly influential report, *A Nation at Risk* (National Commission on Excellence in Education, 1983, p. 5), indicated that "the educational foundations of American society are presently being eroded by a rising tide of mediocrity that threatens our very future as a nation and a people." The Education Commission of the States in its report, *Action for Excellence* (1983), expressed concern about the decline of excellence in schools, underscored the shortage of qualified teachers and decried the low achievement levels of new teachers entering the profession. *American Education: Making It Work* (Bennett, 1988) recommended that practicing teachers as well as new teachers entering the profession be tested. The stream of reform reports in this decade has provided the impetus for efforts to initiate or legislate fundamental changes in the teaching profession. Many of the recommendations in these reports have resulted in state mandates to regulate admission into teacher education programs and to promote individuals through the ranks of the teaching profession. An increase in the use of tests for selecting and certifying teachers is a major consequence of the reform movement.

This chapter examines assessment policies that mandate the use of testing as a vehicle for reforming the teaching profession and the effects of these policies on access of minority students to the teaching profession. It is questionable whether testing has served to enhance the quality of

NEW DIRECTIONS FOR INSTITUTIONAL RESEARCH, no. 65, Spring 1990 © Jossey-Bass Inc., Publishers

the American teaching force. There is some evidence that suggests it only further diminishes the dwindling pool of minority teacher-candidates during a period when the number of minority school-age students is increasing. As H. L. Mencken noted, for every complex problem, there is a simple, obvious solution which is *wrong* (Soar, Medley, and Coker, 1983). The sad reality of tests for prospective teachers is that minorities are failing these tests in disproportionate numbers. A mandate that results in the exclusion of minorities from any profession ". . . is morally wrong, elitist, and in direct conflict with a democratic society's philosophy of education" (p. 241). Shor (1978, p. 184) succinctly states that "the antidote for education's ills fits the regressive tenor of the times—more traditional courses, more mechanical testing, a lust for 'excellence,' and a token glance at equality."

## Testing and Teacher Demographics

The impact of assessment policies on the minority teacher-candidate pool is gaining significance because of changing demographics in the United States. At the same time that minority populations are increasing in America's schools, minority teachers are becoming a vanishing breed (Scott, 1979; Witty, 1982). The 1987 report of the National Education Association notes that the minority-student population is expected to reach 33 percent by 1995 while the percentage of minority teachers is expected to drop to 5 percent. Table 1 illustrates the disproportionate representation of teachers and students from various racial and ethnic groups in the United States. Whites are the only group with a greater number of teachers than students in the public schools.

Research conducted by the Southern Education Foundation (1988) indicates that the minority teacher-candidate pool is dwindling. In aca-

### Table 1. Representation of Teachers and Students from Various Racial or Ethnic Groups

| Racial or Ethnic Group | Percentage of Children in Public Schools | Percentage of Teachers in Public Schools |
|---|---|---|
| Blacks | 16.2 | 6.9 |
| Latinos | 9.1 | 1.9 |
| Asians / Pacific Islanders | 2.5 | 0.9 |
| American Indian / Alaskan Natives | 0.9 | 0.6 |
| Whites | 71.2 | 89.6 |

Source: American Association of Colleges in Teacher Education, 1987 (OERI, 1987a; NEA, 1987).

demic year 1980–81, Blacks and Latinos earned 17 percent of the baccalaureate degrees in education. By 1984–85, this figure decreased to 10.4 percent. Certainly these data are cause for alarm, but the pipeline to provide future teachers presents even more dismal numbers. According to Tracy Robinson (1989) in 1980, 283,000 18- and 19-year-old Black high school graduates entered college; four years later, only 57,000, or 21 percent, were awarded degrees.

The 1986 report of the American College Testing program states that among minority undergraduates selecting a major, teaching is not only chosen less frequently than careers in other fields, but is not among the choices of those who are as yet "undecided" on a major. Further exacerbating the "pipeline" dilemma is the fact that academically talented women and minorities, who in the past preferred teaching as a college major and profession, are now selecting other, more exciting professions that offer better salaries, better working conditions, and more opportunities for advancement (Reed, 1988).

Table 2 illustrates that in Mississippi, Blacks comprise 51 percent of the public-school population, while only 22.9 percent of the teacher-education students are Black. In Indiana, Blacks comprise 18 percent of the children enrolled in public schools but only 1.7 percent of the teacher-education students. Similar imbalances are noted for Georgia and Wisconsin. Perhaps mandatory admission and licensing tests are also contributing to the small number of students entering teacher-education programs.

Martin Haberman (1988) stressed that all children should be afforded the opportunity to experience a realistic representation of American society among the teachers who educate and socialize them. A teaching force which does not reflect the ethnic diversity of the society may send negative messages to White as well as non-White children. Current research provides evidence that Black children could easily have as few as two Black teachers in their elementary- and secondary-school experience. Minority teachers serve as role models and provide minority students motivation to achieve in school, so that these students, like their teachers, can aspire to positions of respect and authority (Nicklos and Brown, 1989; Southern Education Foundation, 1988).

## Test Use and Validity

Rudner and McKinney (1987) reported that, as of April 1987, every state except Alaska and Iowa had either implemented or was planning to implement some form of teacher-testing program. The most prevalent forms of teacher testing include admissions testing and certification testing. Tables 3 and 4 contain summaries of state level testing activities.

Tests used for admitting students to teacher education programs are

**Table 2.  Enrollment Figures for Undergraduate Teacher Preparation
Programs and K-12 Public Schools by Race or Ethnicity
for Selected States**

| | Enrollment in Undergraduate Teacher Preparation Programs by Race or Ethnicity (Percentage) | Enrollment in Public Elementary and Secondary Schools by Race or Ethnicity (Percentage) |
|---|---|---|
| Wisconsin | | |
| Black | 1.8 | 18.0 |
| Latino | — | 3.0 |
| Asian | — | 2.0 |
| N. American | — | 2.0 |
| Other | — | N/A |
| White | 96.0 | 75.0 |
| Indiana | | |
| Black | 1.7 | 18.0 |
| Latino | — | 2.0 |
| Asian | — | 1.0 |
| N. American | — | — |
| Other | — | N/A |
| White | 96.6 | 79.0 |
| Georgia | | |
| Black | 8.8 | 37.0 |
| Latino | — | 1.0 |
| Asian | — | 1.0 |
| N. American | — | — |
| Other | — | N/A |
| White | 89.9 | 62.0 |
| Mississippi | | |
| Black | 22.9 | 51.0 |
| Latino | — | — |
| Asian | — | 1.0 |
| N. American | — | — |
| Other | — | N/A |
| White | 76.4 | 48.0 |

*Note:* Percentages may not equal 100% due to rounding. — = less than 1.0%.
*Sources:* AACTE Minority Teacher Education Enrollment Survey, 1987; Elementary and Secondary Civil Rights Survey; U.S. Department of Education, 1987.

**Table 3. A Summary of Testing for Admissions to Teacher Education Programs**

| State | Test | Passing Scores | Pass Rate % | Other Tests | Education Graduates | Implementation In Place | When |
|---|---|---|---|---|---|---|---|
| Alabama | Custom | | 80 | C | 1,900 | X | |
| Arizona | PPST | 173, 172, 174 | 79 | C | 2,154 | X | |
| California | C-BEST | | 77 | C | 9,562 | X | |
| Colorado | CAT | 75 percentile | 58 | C | 2,361 | X | |
| Connecticut | Custom | | 55 | C | 2,491 | X | |
| Florida | SAT or ACT | 40 percentile | — | C, P | 2,170 | X | |
| Indiana | — | | — | C | 3,750 | | — |
| Kentucky | CTBS | 12.5 GES | 63 | C, P | 1,200 | X | |
| Louisiana | NTE | -, 645, 644 | N/A | C | 1,820 | X | |
| Mississippi | COMP | | N/A | C | 1,689 | X | |
| Missouri | SAT, ACT | 800, 18 | — | | 2,758 | X | |
| Nebraska | PPST | 170, 171, 172 | — | C | 2,253 | | 1987 |
| Nevada | PPST | 169, 169, 170 | 95 | C | 258 | X | |
| New Mexico | Misc. | | N/A | C | — | X | |
| North Carolina | NTE | 636, 631, 644 | N/A | C, P | 4,500 | X | |
| North Dakota | Misc. | | — | C | 950 | X | |
| Ohio | — | | — | C | 5,829 | | 1987 |
| Oklahoma | Misc. | | — | C, P | 2,400 | X | |
| Oregon | C-BEST | | 77 | C | 1,700 | X | |
| South Carolina | Custom | | 67 | C, P | 1,282 | X | |
| Tennessee | PPST | 169, 169, 172 | N/A | C | 4,000 | X | |
| Texas | PPST | 171, 172, 173 | 71 | C, P, R | 10,000 | X | |
| Utah | Misc. | | N/A | | 1,842 | X | |
| Washington | Custom, SAT, ACT | 80, 700, 16 | N/A | | 2,007 | X | |
| West Virginia | PPST, COMP | 172, 172, 171, 17 | 68 | C | 2,017 | X | |
| Wisconsin | PPST | | — | C | 2,819 | | 1989 |
| Wyoming | CAT | 70 percentile | N/A | | 300 | X | |
| Totals | 27 | | Mean = 7.2% | 24, 6, 1 | | 23 | 4 |

Source: Rudner and McKinney, 1987, p. 44.

# Table 4. A Summary of State Teacher-Certification Programs

| State | Test | Coverage Basic | Coverage Prof. | Coverage Subj. | Passing Scores | Pass Rate | Other Tests | Number of Teachers | Emergency Certification | Implementation In Place | Implementation When |
|---|---|---|---|---|---|---|---|---|---|---|---|
| Alabama | Custom | | X | X | | 85 | A | 36,000 | .2 | X | |
| Arizona | Custom | X | X | | | 78 | A | 28,895 | N/A | X | |
| Arkansas | NTE | X | X | | | — | R | 24,085 | <.1 | | — |
| California | C-BEST | X | | | | 74 | A | 179,660 | 3.4 | X | |
| Colorado | — | | | | | — | A | 29,895 | <.1 | | 1987 |
| Connecticut | NTE | | | X | | — | A | 32,467 | .2 | | 1987 |
| Delaware | PPST | X | | | 175, 175, 172 | 69 | | 5,516 | 5.3 | X | |
| Florida | Custom | X | X | | | 85 | A, P | 86,223 | 11.6 | X | |
| Georgia | Custom | X | | X | | 78 | P, R | 56,321 | 17.6 | X | |
| Hawaii | NTE | X | X | X | 647, 651, 648 | 73 | | 9,060 | .3 | X | |
| Idaho | NTE | X | X | | | — | | 10,160 | N/A | | — |
| Illinois | Custom | X | | X | | — | | 100,497 | N/A | | 1988 |
| Indiana | NTE | X | X | X | 647, 653, 646 | 88 | A | 49,646 | .8 | X | |
| Kansas | PPST, NTE | X | X | | 168, 168, 170 | 94 | | 26,260 | 0 | X | |
| Kentucky | NTE | X | | X | 637, 643, 641 | 93 | A, P | 32,400 | <.1 | X | |
| Louisiana | NTE | X | | X | 644, 645, 645 | 87 | A | 46,840 | .7 | X | |
| Maine | NTE | X | X | | | — | | 12,510 | 3.3 | | 1988 |
| Maryland | NTE | X | X | | | — | | 38,029 | .7 | | 1987 |
| Massachusetts | — | X | | | | — | | 56,333 | .2 | | 1989 |
| Michigan | — | X | | X | | — | | 88,000 | <.1 | | 1991 |
| Minnesota | PPST | X | | X | 173, 169, 172 | — | | 41,444 | .2 | | 1988 |
| Mississippi | NTE | X | X | | 639, 644, 642 | 88 | | 24,772 | 4.2 | X | |
| Missouri | — | | | X | | — | A | 47,240 | 4.7 | | 1987 |

| State | Test | | | | Test forms | % | Use | N | % | | Year |
|---|---|---|---|---|---|---|---|---|---|---|---|
| Montana | NTE | X | X | | 644, 648, 648 | 92 | | 22,028 | 0 | X | 1987 |
| Nebraska | PPST | X | | | 170, 171, 172 | — | A | 17,513 | <.1 | | 1990 |
| Nevada | PPST | X | | X | | — | A | 7,751 | 0 | | |
| New Hampshire | PPST | X | | | 173, 174, 173 | 74 | | 10,104 | 1.3 | X | |
| New Jersey | NTE | X | | X | 644, –, – | 83 | | 72,858 | 2.7 | X | |
| New Mexico | NTE | X | X | X | 645, 644, 630 | 88 | A | 14,200 | 5.6 | X | |
| New York | NTE | X | X | X | 649, 650, 646 | 79 | | 164,900 | 2.4 | X | |
| North Carolina | NTE | X | X | X | 631, 636, 644 | 80 | A, P | 56,084 | N/A | | |
| North Dakota | — | | | | | — | A | 8,794 | <.1 | | |
| Ohio | — | X | X | X | | — | A | 87,729 | 1.0 | | 1987 |
| Oklahoma | Custom | | | X | | 81 | A | 35,000 | 1.7 | | X |
| Oregon | C-BEST | X | | | | 80 | A | 24,413 | 2.0 | | X |
| Pennsylvania | NTE | X | X | X | | — | A | 101,150 | .2 | | 1987 |
| Rhode Island | NTE | X | X | | 649, 657, 648 | N/A | | 7,548 | .2 | | X |
| South Carolina | NTE, Custom | | X | X | | N/A | A, P | 36,935 | N/A | X | |
| South Dakota | NTE | X | X | X | | — | | 8,022 | 1.3 | X | |
| Tennessee | NTE | X | X | X | 640, 644, 635 | N/A | | 40,000 | N/A | X | |
| Texas | Custom | | | X | | 85 | A, P, R | 185,000 | N/A | X | |
| Virginia | NTE | X | X | X | 639, 649, 639 | N/A | P | 56,863 | 0 | X | |
| West Virginia | Custom | | | X | | 83 | A | 22,557 | 5.9 | X | |
| Wisconsin | — | | | X | | — | A | 45,350 | 2.4 | | 1987 |
| Totals | 44 | 31 | 24 | 29 | | Mean = 83% | 22, 7, 3 | | | 26 | 18 |

Source: Rudner and McKinney, 1987, p. 44.

in place in twenty-seven states. The Pre-Professional Skills Test (PPST) is the most frequently used admissions test. Other tests used for admission include the Scholastic Aptitude Test (SAT), the American College Testing Program's College Admission Test, and custom-made tests.

Forty-four states are currently testing prospective teachers as a certification requirement. The NTE (formerly the National Teacher Examination) is the most frequently used test for certification. Other tests that are used include the Pre-Professional Skills Test (PPST), the California Basic Education Skills Tests (C-BEST), and custom-made tests.

Arkansas, Georgia, and Texas are testing or have recently tested practicing teachers for recertification, utilizing custom-made tests. New teachers are assessed through formal observation in several states: Florida, Georgia, Kentucky, North Carolina, South Carolina, and Virginia. These programs are designed to provide assistance to beginning teachers and ultimately result in the determination of whether or not the teacher will receive regular certification.

While one might argue that teacher-competency tests measure mastery of basic knowledge reflected in the typical general-education curriculum in many colleges, several issues undermine that argument. First, no agreement exists on the specific content necessary for teaching. Different states use different tests and varying passing scores (Anrig, Baratz-Snowden, and Goertz, 1987; Gifford, 1986). Furthermore, where the same test is used in different states, validity studies indicate that the knowledge base deemed critical for teaching differs according to the professional opinions and training-program philosophies of those participating in the validation studies. For example, the NTE Core Battery test was designed by the Educational Testing Service (ETS) with the assistance of teacher educators and teaching practitioners who judged the validity of the test items (Anrig, 1986). While ETS adhered to what it deemed strict standards of test quality and fairness, including a request to such independent groups as the National Education Association and American Federation of Teachers to select multiracial panel members to judge these standards, Gifford (1987, p. 21) notes a critical problem with this approach:

> the Core Battery is purported to represent a consensus among educators as to the knowledge important to an entry level teacher. However, in fact, there is little agreement among practitioners and researchers as to what beginning teachers need to know. The judgments of ETS panelists about test-item validity may therefore have been situational, subjective and idiosyncratic. In implicit recognition of this probability, ETS requires each state that chooses to administer the NTE to conduct its own content-validity study. However, this policy does not increase confidence in the NTE's validity. Using the same basic methodology described above, ETS itself has conducted 60 percent (21) of the state

studies. While as many as 38 percent of the test items have been identified as invalid for a given state, the NTE has not been modified accordingly, but continues to be administered as originally designed.

A second important issue is that the predictive validity of the competency tests has not been substantiated. The tests do not differentiate those who will become effective from those who will become ineffective teachers. According to Stedman (1984), the greatest value of a test lies in its predictive validity, or its accuracy in determining who is likely to succeed or fail in professional practice. Stedman cautions that a rigorous plan to evaluate both predictive validity and social impact is particularly crucial in the case of legislated decisions which are likely to remain in force for long periods of time. Without such a plan, potential discrimination cannot be corrected because it will be unnoticed and undocumented. Research on the ability of teacher-competency tests to predict success in the classroom is scarce (Gifford, 1986; Smith, 1984; Stedman, 1984).

A case in point that demonstrates the lack of predictive validity and the need for caution in the use of existing competency tests is a Virginia study of assessment of actual classroom performance of new teachers. A Fall 1985 report of the results of Virginia's Beginning Teacher Assistance Program (BTAP), which measures fourteen skills that new teachers must demonstrate to be certified, indicates no significant racial differences in the evaluations. Despite evidence that Black collegians in Virginia have failed the NTE twice as often as Whites, 57 percent of new Black teachers passed the BTAP classroom evaluation compared with 55 percent of new White teachers. Michael Caldwell, who headed the Virginia study, noted that the findings confirm what Black educators have contended throughout the United States in the thirty-five states that require a written certification test: "Blacks can teach as well as Whites, though their educational background may make it harder for them to pass standardized tests" ("Evaluation," 1986, p. 1).

Gifford (1987, p. 21) notes the following:

> the content of the Core Battery appears to be more closely related to the curricula of teacher-preparation programs than to the competency of effective beginning teachers. According to ETS the tests provide information on knowledge and skills the candidate acquired through a teacher education program. Especially in light of the manifest need to reform teacher education programs, it cannot be assumed that the objectives and content of teacher-training curricula reflect the proficiency areas or levels possessed by capable entry-level teachers. That this concern has substance is supported by ETS's recent undertaking of a job analysis study involving 16,000 practicing teachers. Presumably, the results will be used to increase the job relatedness of the NTE.

A third issue in the rush to legislate the use of tests of teacher competency has been controversy regarding the belief that teaching requires skill in the basics of reading, writing, and mathematics, competence in subject matter, and knowledge of and ability to use general pedagogical skills. Shulman contends that a teacher assessment limited to these three areas of educational experience "trivializes teaching, ignores its complexities and diminishes demands" (1987, p. 318). This content is supported by those who believe that beyond any demonstration of content knowledge as evidenced by performance on comprehensive examinations, one must consider other variables such as the personal characteristics of effective teachers. The teacher-competency tests do not measure affective characteristics. Shulman notes that specific qualities and understandings, skills and abilities, and traits and sensibilities are characteristic of competent teachers.

## Test Impact on Minority Teachers

The use of competency testing has not proven to be a viable strategy to improve the quality of the American teaching force, but it has served to reduce the number of minority teachers. Smith (1987, pp. 245–246) summarizes the impact of competency testing on minorities as follows:

> [A]lmost without exception, cut scores have been recommended or established, regardless of examination, at the precise point that eliminates a majority of the Black and Hispanic candidates but permits most White candidates to pass. . . . The teacher competency testing programs were designed to ensure excellence in teaching. Yet they will have negligible effect on changing the quality of the majority White teaching force of the past. In the next decade, testing will maintain the status quo rather than introduce an important innovation for achieving excellence. Testing appears to guarantee the elimination of minority teachers in a decade when they will be sorely needed.

On the national level, disproportionate numbers of minorities are failing teacher-certification examinations. This does not mean that minorities lack the intellectual or job-performance abilities to become effective teachers. The use of traditional standardized tests seems rather to be a deliberate effort to exclude minorities from the teaching profession (Smith, 1987). In a comprehensive study, Anrig, Baratz-Snowden, and Goertz (1987) found that if the highest state qualifying score on the NTE Test of Communication Skills (653) were applied to the entire NTE candidate pool, 80 percent of Whites would qualify to become teachers as compared with only 25 percent of the Black and 46 percent of the Latino candidates. If the lowest qualifying score (636) were applied, nearly all of the Whites would pass while nearly 30 percent of Black and 15 percent of Latino examinees would be eliminated from the teaching pool. They found similar results for the Test of General Knowledge and the Test of Professional Knowledge. Ninety-five percent of the Whites tested score at or above the lower score, as compared with 80 percent of the Blacks and 92 percent of the Latinos.

Anrig (1987) also points out that minority performance on other comprehensive examinations used for teachers parallels the performance of these groups on the NTE. In California, scores on the California Basic Educational Skills Test (also developed by ETS) indicate an 81-percent pass rate for Whites compared with 46 percent for Latinos, and 33 percent for Blacks. Comparable scores were reported for the Arizona Teacher Proficiency Examination (ATPE) with a 73-percent pass rate for Whites, 40-percent for Latinos, and 31-percent for Blacks. In Oklahoma, however, 79 percent of the White, 83 percent of the Latino, and 48 percent of the Black candidates passed that state's certification test.

In a review of minority performance on teacher-competency tests, Smith (1987) found substantial evidence from states with several years experience using the tests and states completing initial validation studies that disproportionate numbers of minority students are being screened out of teaching. Haney, Madaus, and Kreitzer (1987) argue that the way in which tests are being used with state-mandated cut-scores is discriminating between candidates more on the basis of race than on the basis of any independent measures of teacher quality. Other researchers have reported on the disproportionate impact of teacher-competency testing on minorities (Eissenberg and Rudner, 1988; Ethridge, 1979; Garcia, 1985 and 1986; Goertz and Pitcher, 1985; Graham, 1987; Jackson and Pressman, 1988; Scott, 1979; Witty, 1982; Wynn, 1984).

From a historical perspective, Smith (1987) reports that a pattern of excluding minority teachers existed prior to the testing movement, which began in a small band of southern states. In this same region, massive displacement of black teachers occurred after the 1954 Brown decision. The first states to test for teacher competency include the twelve southern and border states (known as Adams states after *Adams* v. *Richardson*) required by federal mandate to desegregate their public colleges and universities.

In addressing the question why minority students are failing teacher tests, the literature only gives minimal attention to the broader issues that include historical precedents and socioeconomic factors related to the education of disadvantaged people. Graham (1987, p. 600) notes that poor performance on the tests in the southern states provides

a graphic illustration of a problem that is endemic in sections of the U.S. that have high concentrations of poor families, particularly when racial differences affect that concentration. The children of the poor and of racial minorities are likely to do less well than children from more afflu- ent families. . . . There have been gross disparities between expenditures for the education of black children and expenditures for the education of white children and children of the rich and of the poor which were main- tained well into the 1960's. Poverty is a predictor of academic performance because the circumstances of poverty often erode supportive family and community structures that would likely enhance learning.

## Suggestions for Change

Smith (1984) describes testing of teachers and prospective teachers as the single most visible national response to public mandates for reform in American education. But for teachers and those who would become teachers the response has a high price: "The use of competency tests to certify teachers has forced educators and the public to challenge the most cherished premise underlying the philosophy of education in a demo- cratic society: that persons regardless of social economic status, race, or creed are guaranteed both excellence and equity in their pursuit of educa- tion" (p. 6). With the mandate for competency testing of teachers, legis- latures and state departments of education have reduced excellence to a single dimension—performance on paper-and-pencil tests—whose rele- vance for subsequent successful and effective performance in the class- room is questionable and debatable.

In view of the fact that across the nation, the polity has deemed teacher-competency testing a necessary vehicle to promote excellence in American education, in spite of its impact on minorities, educators on all levels must work collaboratively to ensure the participation of minor- ities in teaching. The teaching profession and teacher-training insti- tutions, in collaboration with policy makers, must contribute to the solutions. As Haberman (1988) notes, all children should be afforded the opportunity to experience a realistic representation of society among their teachers. Efforts must be made to ensure this goal. If the society is serious about equity and excellence in the education of all children, and if the society is correct in believing that the education and preparation of teachers is of paramount importance, then there are both long-term and short-term strategies that must be effected.

First, over the long-term, policy makers must be willing to affirm their commitment to excellence *with equity* through funding to improve the quality of the public schools from which the minority teacher-candi- date pool is drawn. The education of all children, and particularly those from minority and low-income families, must be improved. As columnist William Rasberry of the *Washington Post* succinctly states: ". . . the rea- son minority applicants fare worse on the tests than whites is that they themselves are the victims of inferior schooling" (Gifford, 1987, p. 22). The inference can be drawn that the results of teacher-competency tests indicate that the elementary and secondary education of the nation's youth must be strengthened. Greater focus on the preparation of students from kindergarten through twelfth grade is needed to help minority students gain a firm intellectual foundation and strong knowledge base before they enter college. Hatton (1988, p. 68) notes: "Simply put, minority groups must have more effective schools in order to produce more college applicants—and more successful college students."

In the short-term and until such time as minority students enter college with the requisite educational foundations—reading, writing, basic mathematical computations, reasoning, and critical thinking skills—to succeed on comprehensive examinations and in their chosen professions, colleges have an obligation to prepare these students to be successful at doing college-level work. And government has an obligation to increase funding to schools and colleges of education to implement quality programs, including preparation for competency exams. Excellent models to improve test performance exist at a number of colleges. These programs have demonstrated that students achieve success on competency tests if a concerted effort is made to strengthen students' basic skills and test-sophistication skills and if students are taught what they need to know. In 1985, the Virginia General Assembly appropriated $500,000 to Norfolk State University, a predominantly Black institution, over a period of two years to develop such a program. The results indicate that the pass rate of teacher-education students on the NTE jumped from 28 percent in 1982 to more than 80 percent in June 1989 (Witty, 1989). A similar program at Grambling State University in Louisiana, also predominantly Black, resulted in an increase in the NTE pass rate for teacher-education students from 5 percent to 85 percent (Spencer, 1986). This does not mean that colleges should strive for minimal competency levels. It simply provides a means for colleges to aid minorities until public elementary and secondary education improve as evidenced by the ability of disadvantaged minority youth to meet and exceed the new standards for entry to the teaching profession. Other short-term recommendations include the following:

• Expand evaluation of teacher competence beyond the single method of "paper-and-pencil" tests. Give more attention to performance-based evaluation and to the personal qualities that characterize effective teachers. Policy makers, state department-of-education personnel, teachers, and teacher trainers should collaborate to develop additional strategies.

• Increase federal and state scholarship programs for minority students who are pursuing careers in teaching. The state of Virginia has recently expanded its teacher-scholarship program, previously designed to prepare teachers in subject areas with critical shortages, to include all qualified minority students.

• Increase collaboration between public schools and colleges to establish early identification programs to encourage an interest in teaching and to strengthen the academic skills of minority students who wish to pursue careers in teaching. These programs may start as early as middle school with teacher cadet programs and continue through high schools with Future Educators of America Clubs. Summer enrichment programs held on college campuses to enhance and strengthen academic skills and provide exposure to different test formats and test-sophistication skills might be implemented. Mentorship programs in which college students serve as mentors and tutors for low-income minority middle and high school students can increase the interest of such students in and aspiration toward higher education and, ultimately, careers in teaching. Parental involvement seems critical to the success of these efforts. Parents, particularly low-income minority parents, need to know that students who aspire to attend college must pursue an academic track in high school. Further, parents should be made aware of financial-aid packages and scholarships that will ease the burden of college expenses.

• Beyond high school, community colleges provide a rich resource from which to recruit and prepare minorities for the teaching profession. Over half of all minority students enrolled in college are in the community colleges (Haberman, 1988). Articulation agreements between two-year and four- and five-year teacher-training institutions provide an opportunity to recruit and to prepare minority students for the teaching profession.

An agenda for institutional researchers who wish to address this issue might include the following items:

• Study of the extent to which the tests currently in use differentiate between prospective teachers on the basis of teacher competence rather than on the basis of race.

• Study of the effectiveness of teachers hired prior to a testing requirement and those who were tested and certified.

• Study of the factors that account for the fact that minority students appear not to have passing rates on teacher tests that are comparable to White students, even when they attend the same teacher-education program. The existing research, which indicates that the type of institution has little bearing on test performance of minority-teacher candidates, is limited. Research on the reasons for this phenomenon is even more scarce.

• Design a model for articulation and collaboration between historically Black four-year teacher-training institutions and historically White institutions offering extended teacher education programs culminating in a graduate degree in education.

• Given the paucity of retention research on minority college students, study what are the factors that encourage minority students to persist in college to earn a teaching degree. What are the characteristics of these students, and how well do they perform in the classroom? What factors explain why some minority students do not persist in teacher-training programs?

In summary, testing has not enhanced the quality of the American teaching force. In fact, it has had negligible effect on the quality of the White teacher force while diminishing the minority teacher-candidate pool. The new assessment policies and practices that exclude minorities from the teaching profession are in direct conflict with the ideals of education in a democratic society. Now in place, these policies are not likely to change in the foreseeable future. The challenge is two-fold. First, we must continue to recruit and retain a representative group of qualified minorities in teaching to serve as role models for *all* of our children. Second, elementary and secondary education must strive toward better preparation of future teachers. Once these hurdles are passed, we can move on to even higher standards that are meaningful to all groups in our pluralistic society and that will have a true and positive impact on the quality of American education.

## References

Anrig, G. R. "Teacher Education and Teacher Testing: The Rush to Mandate." *Phi Delta Kappan*, 1986, *67* (6), 447–451.

Anrig, G. R., Baratz-Snowden, J., and Goertz, M. E. "Testing Policies and Minority Participation in Teaching: A Look at the Research." Paper presented at the annual meeting of the American Education Research Association, Washington, D.C., April 1987.

Bennett, W. J. *American Education: Making It Work*. Washington, D.C.: U.S. Department of Education, 1988.

Eissenberg, T. E., and Rudner, L. "State Testing of Teachers: A Summary." *Journal of Teacher Education*, 1988, *39* (4), 21–22.

Ethridge, S. B. "Impact of the 1954 *Brown* v. *Topeka Board of Education* Decision on Black Educators." *Negro Educational Review*, 1979, *30* (4), 217–232.

"Evaluation Shows Black and White Teacher Skills Equal: Virginia Results Diminish Validity of Test Use." *Black Issues in Higher Education*, 1986, *3* (2), 1.

Garcia, P. A. "A Study on Teacher Competency Testing and Test Validity with Implications for Minorities and the Results and Implications of the Use of the Pre-Professional Skills Test (PPST) as a Screening Device for Entrance into Teacher Education Programs in Texas." Washington, D.C.: National Institute of Education, 1985.

Garcia, P. A. "The Impact of National Testing on Ethnic Minorities: With Proposed Solutions." *Journal of Negro Education*, 1986, *55* (3), 347–357.

Gifford, B. "Excellence and Equity." In L. M. Rudner and K. C. McKinney (eds.), *What's Happening in Teacher Testing*. Washington, D.C.: Office of Educational Research and Improvement, 1987.

Giroux, H. A., and McLaren, P. "Teacher Education and the Policies of Engagement: The Case for Democratic Schooling." *Harvard Educational Review*, 1987, *56* (3), 213–238.

Goertz, M. E., and Pitcher, B. *The Impact of NTE Use by States on Teacher Selection.* Princeton, N.J.: Educational Testing Service, 1985.

Graham, P. A. "Black Teachers: A Drastically Scarce Resource." *Phi Delta Kappan,* 1987, *68* (8), 598–605.

Haberman, M. "Alliances Between Four-Year Institutions and Two-Year Colleges Can Help Recruit Minority Students into Teaching." *Chronicle of Higher Education,* July 27, 1988, p. A28.

Haney, W., Madaus, G., and Kreitzer, A. "Charms Talismanic: Testing Teachers for the Improvement of American Education." In E. R. Kopf (ed.), *Review of Research in Education.* Washington, D.C.: American Education Research Association, 1987.

Hatton, B. "A Game Plan for Ending the Minority Teacher Shortage." *NEA Today,* 1988, *6* (6), 66–69.

Jackson, N., and Pressman, H. "Increasing the Number of Minority Teachers: Directions for State Policy." Atlanta, Ga.: Southern Education Foundation, 1988.

Messick, S., and Anderson, S. "Educational Testing, Individual Development, and Social Responsibility." *Counseling Psychologist,* 1970, *2* (2), 80–87.

National Commission on Excellence in Education. *A Nation at Risk.* Washington, D.C.: U.S. Department of Education, 1983.

Nicklos, L. B., and Brown, W. S. "Recruiting Minorities into the Teaching Profession: An Educational Imperative." *Educational Horizons,* 1989, *67,* 145–149.

Reed, D. F. "Wanted: More Teacher Education Students." *Action in Teacher Education,* 1988, *88* (1), 31–36.

Robinson, T. "Keeping More Means Losing Less." *Black Issues in Higher Education,* 1989, *5* (23), 76.

Rudner, L. M. "Teacher Testing—An Update." *Educational Measurement Issues and Practice,* 1988, *7* (1), 16–19.

Rudner, L. M., and McKinney, K. C. "State by State Descriptions." In L. M. Rudner and K. C. McKinney (eds.), *What's Happening in Teacher Testing.* Washington, D.C.: Office of Educational Research and Improvement, 1987.

Sandefur, J. T. "State Reactions to Competency Assessment in Teacher Education." In B. Boardman and M. Butler (eds.), *Competency Assessment in Teacher Education: Making It Work.* Washington, D.C.: American Association of Colleges in Teacher Education, 1981. (ED 206 570)

Sandefur, J. T. *Standards for Admission to Teacher Education Programs.* Saint Paul: Minnesota Higher Education Coordinating Board, 1984. (ED 251 417)

Scott, H. J. *Minimum-Competency Testing: The Newest Obstruction to the Education of Black and Other Disadvantaged Americans.* Princeton, N.J.: ERIC Clearinghouse on Tests, Measurement, and Evaluation, 1979. (ED 178 618)

Shor, I. "Equality Is Excellence: Transforming Teacher Education and the Learning Process." *Harvard Educational Review,* 1987, *56* (4), 406–426.

Short, E. C. "The Concept of Competence: Its Use and Misuse in Education." *Journal of Teacher Education,* 1985, *36* (2), 2–6.

Shulman, L. S. "Knowledge and Teaching: Foundations of the New Reform." *Harvard Educational Review,* 1987, *56,* (4), 313–334.

Smith, G. P. "The Critical Issue of Excellence and Equity in Competency Testing." *Journal of Teacher Education,* 1984, *35* (2), 6–9.

Smith, G. P. "The Impact of Competency Tests on Teacher Education: Ethical and Legal Issues in Selecting and Certifying Teachers." In M. Haberman and J. M. Backus (eds.), *Advances in Teacher Education.* Vol. 3. Norwood, N.J.: Ablex, 1987.

Soar, R., Medley, D. M., and Coker, H. "Teacher Evaluation: A Critique of Currently Used Methods." *Phi Delta Kappan*, 1983, *65* (7), 239-246.
Southern Education Foundation. *Increasing the Number of Minority Teachers.* (Filmstrip.) Atlanta, Ga.: Southern Regional Task Force Report, 1988.
Spencer, T. L. "Teacher Education at Grambling State University: A Move Toward Excellence." *Journal of Negro Education*, 1986, *55* (3), 293-303.
Stedman, C. H. "Testing for Competency: A Pyrrhic Victory?" *Journal of Teacher Education*, 1984, *35* (2), 2-5.
Task Force on Education for Economic Growth. *Action for Excellence.* Denver, Colo.: Education Commission of the States, 1983.
Witty, E. P. *Prospects for Black Teachers: Preparation, Certification, Employment.* Washington, D.C.: ERIC Clearinghouse on Teacher Education, 1982. (ED 213 659)
Witty, E. P. "Increasing the Pool of Black Teachers: Plans and Strategies." In A. Garibaldi (ed.), *Teacher Recruitment and Retention with Special Focus on Minority Teachers.* Washington, D.C.: National Education Association, 1989.
Wynn, C. "The Technology of Teacher Competency Testing." In M. David (ed.), *Prospective Black Teachers and the Closing Door: Strategies for Entry.* Birmingham: Alabama Center for Higher Education, 1984. (ED 255 476)

*Diane J. Simon is assistant dean of the School of Education, Virginia Commonwealth University.*

*Misconceptions about Asian and Pacific American students abound. This chapter discusses and explains their performance on several assessment measures and provides recommendations for future assessment efforts.*

# Assessing the Educational Performance of Minority Students: The Case of Asian and Pacific Americans

*Jean J. Endo*

This chapter discusses how Asian and Pacific Americans perform on several general assessment measures being used by institutions of higher education, the reasons they perform as they do, and some recommendations for future assessment efforts. The performance on various types of assessment measures by students of any minority background should be examined within an interpretive framework that is, to a certain degree, specific to that background. The case of Asian and Pacific Americans (hereafter referred to as Asians) will be used to illustrate this point.

Asians have been given much less attention in the assessment literature than Blacks and Latinos, and there are many misconceptions about Asians, in particular that they are all superior students who experience no problems in higher education. Therefore, this chapter is also designed to convey some basic information about the status of Asian college students.

Assessment encompasses institutional measures of students' academic potential and learning as they relate to program objectives. Colleges and universities conduct assessments in a variety of ways. The discussion in

I would like to express my appreciation to Marsha Hirano-Nakanishi, Samuel Peng, Amefil Agbayani, Phyllis Edamatsu, and Russell Endo for their comments on an earlier draft of this chapter.

this chapter will be guided by Turnbull's hypothetical pattern of assessment programs (Turnbull, 1985), and the assessment measures to be examined will include college admissions tests; high school and college gradepoint averages; college participation, persistence, and graduation rates; and measures from institutional surveys of students' perceptions of their educational outcomes and their college environment. Many institutions use achievement examinations given during the college years as assessment measures, but these will not be covered in this chapter because very little information about Asians in terms of such examinations is available.

## Historical and Social Background

Asians are the fastest growing minority group in the United States. The 1980 census counted 3.3 million, a 128 percent increase over 1970, and the population is expected to grow to 10 million by the year 2000. A majority of Asians live in Hawaii and on the West Coast, although there are large populations in other areas of the country, notably the Midwest and Northeast. In the fall of 1986, 448,000 Asians were enrolled in higher education institutions, an increase of 126 percent from 1976; by the year 2000, this number is expected to increase to over 900,000 (Peng, 1988; Suzuki, 1988).

The term "Asian and Pacific American" covers several groups, each originally from a society with distinct cultural, social, and economic patterns. Asian groups include the Chinese, Japanese, Filipinos, Koreans, Native Hawaiians, Guamanians, Samoans, Vietnamese, Cambodians, Laotians, Hmong, East Indians, and other Pacific Island, South Asian, and Southeast Asian peoples.

The Chinese were the first sizeable Asian group to migrate to America. Most of them arrived during the late 1840s through the first few decades of the twentieth century. The Chinese were followed by the Japanese (largely from 1880-1924), Koreans (1902-1905), and Filipinos (primarily during the 1920s and early 1930s). By the mid-1930s, large-scale immigration had virtually ceased because of restrictive laws, but small numbers of Asians from several societies continued to come. With the enactment of more liberal immigration policies in 1965, large numbers of Asians—particularly Chinese, Filipinos, and Koreans—have migrated to the U.S. Also, since the fall of Saigon in 1975, several hundred thousand Vietnamese, Cambodian, Laotian, and Hmong refugees have arrived.

Partly because of these diverse migration patterns, the historical experiences of Asian groups have been very different. In addition, Asians · today vary widely in their degree of economic and social adaptation to American society and in their contemporary experiences—variations best exemplified by comparing the fourth or fifth generation descendants of the earliest immigrants with the newest arrivals.

Another general difference between Asian groups is in socioeconomic status. For example, in 1980, Japanese, Chinese, and Filipino families had higher median incomes than those of Koreans, Native Hawaiians, Samoans, Guamanians, and Vietnamese (U.S. Bureau of the Census, 1980). Socioeconomic status is also one source of difference within Asian groups. These groups differ on income by the nativity, gender, age, and occupation of income earners. Native-born Chinese adults, for instance, have higher average incomes than foreign-born Chinese adults (Cabezas and Kawaguchi, 1988). In terms of education, Japanese have, overall, the highest levels of educational attainment. On the other hand, a large percentage of Hmong adults have had no formal education.

## Performance on Assessment Measures

Asian groups are obviously very diverse. This diversity has implications for the progress of Asian students in higher education in the United States. Ideally, assessment data should be collected and reported for individual Asian groups. Unfortunately, most institutions and researchers collect or report only aggregated data. The following discussion examines how Asians perform on several assessment measures. It is limited to the extent that it must rely on available aggregated data. Examples will be presented where possible for individual groups, although most of the available data come from a handful of large research universities.

*College Admissions Tests.* In the aggregate, Asians tend to perform better than Whites on the mathematical portions of standardized college admissions tests but not as well on the verbal portions. In 1989, Asians had mean Scholastic Aptitude Test (SAT) math and verbal scores of 525 and 409, respectively, compared with 491 and 446 for Whites; on the math and English sections of the American College Test (ACT), Asians had mean scores of 21.2 and 18.5, respectively, compared with 17.9 and 19.2 for Whites (Dodge, 1989).

There are some differences between individual Asian groups on test scores. For instance, data on the 1984 freshmen at the eight University of California campuses, the freshman cohorts from 1979 through 1982 at the University of Hawaii, Manoa, and the combined 1980–1982 freshman cohorts at the University of California, Berkeley, suggest that Filipinos, Native Hawaiians, and Southeast Asians tend to get lower SAT math and verbal scores than Japanese, Chinese, and Koreans (Sue and Abe, 1988; University of Hawaii, Department of Sociology, 1988; Frank, 1988). Further, the 1984 University of California data show that, within each Asian group, females had lower mean verbal and math scores than males.

*High School Grade-Point Average and Class Rank.* When viewed collectively, Asians tend to have slightly higher high school grade-point averages (GPAs) and class rankings than those for Whites. In 1985, college-bound Asian seniors who participated in the College Board's Admissions Testing Program had a mean high school GPA of 3.18 compared to 3.06 for Whites. Also, these Asians had a median class ranking at the eighty-first percentile compared to the seventy-fifth percentile for Whites (Ramist and Arbeiter, 1986).

Again, there are some differences between individual Asian groups. For example, among 1984 freshmen at the eight University of California campuses, Filipinos had the lowest mean high school GPA of all the Asian groups (Sue and Abe, 1988). Among 1985-86 high school juniors and seniors in San Diego, Pacific Islanders, Filipinos, and Southeast Asians had lower mean GPAs than other Asians; and among a sample of San Diego Southeast Asian high school students in 1985, Laotians had the lowest average GPA followed by Cambodians, Hmong, Chinese from Vietnam, and Vietnamese (Rumbaut and Ima, 1988).

*College Participation Rate.* Asians, in the aggregate, tend to have higher college participation rates than Whites. In the national High School and Beyond survey, 86 percent of the 1980 Asian high school seniors enrolled in colleges within two years of their graduation compared to 64 percent of the Whites (Peng, 1988).

However, certain Asian groups tend to have lower college attendance rates than others, in part because of high school attrition. For instance, Native Hawaiian females in Hawaii have a high school dropout rate that is almost twice the state average (University of Hawaii, 1987), and in San Diego high schools in 1985-1986, Pacific Islanders and Cambodians had much higher dropout rates than other Asians (Rumbaut and Ima, 1988). A recent policy study of immigrant students in the California public schools identifies Filipinos and Southeast Asians as being among the groups most at-risk for dropping out (Olsen, 1988).

While Asians attend colleges and universities throughout the country, two-thirds are concentrated in schools in California, New York, Hawaii, Illinois, and Texas. Recent accounts in the mass media have emphasized the enrollment of Asians in selective institutions, and, indeed, Asians comprise disproportionately high percentages of the students at such schools as the University of California, Berkeley (20 percent); the California Institute of Technology (14 percent); Columbia University (9 percent); Stanford University (8 percent); the University of Chicago (7 percent); and Harvard University (5 percent). However, in 1986, 42 percent of all Asian students were attending two-year colleges and only 14 percent were at private institutions (Peng, 1988).

*College Grade-Point Average.* Asians, when viewed collectively, tend to have college GPAs that are similar to those for Whites. At the eight University of California campuses, 1,984 Asian and White freshmen had mean first-year GPAs of 2.74 and 2.75, respectively (Sue and Abe, 1988), and at the University of Washington, Asians in each of the years from

1982 to 1986 had average GPAs just slightly lower (from 0.06 to 0.10) than those for Whites (Lujan, 1988). The 1981 Asian freshmen at the University of Colorado, Boulder, had a mean first-year GPA of 2.62 compared to 2.66 for Whites (Endo, 1987).

However, there is evidence that suggests that certain Asian groups including Filipinos, Pacific Islanders, and some Southeast Asian groups tend to achieve lower grades than others. As an example, among the 1984 Asian freshmen at the eight University of California campuses, Filipinos had the lowest mean first-year GPA, 2.44; by comparison, the mean for Whites was 2.75 (Sue and Abe, 1988). At the University of Hawaii, Manoa, Filipinos and Native Hawaiians in each of the freshman cohorts from 1979 to 1982 had lower average first-year and final cumulative GPAs (from 0.12 to 0.53 lower) than Japanese as well as the total cohort (University of Hawaii, Department of Sociology, 1988). And, among the 1988 Asian freshmen at the University of Colorado, Boulder, Hmong and Cambodian students had lower mean first-year GPAs than other Southeast Asians as well as other Asians and Whites (Endo, 1989).

*College Persistence Rate.* In the aggregate, Asians tend to have reasonably good college persistence rates. Carroll (1988) studied the persistence in college of Asians using the 1982 high school graduates in the High School and Beyond survey and a simplified model that examines students who enroll full-time in four-year higher educational institutions to pursue bachelor's degrees immediately after graduating from high school. The model focuses on students who continue to pursue full-time studies at the same institution. Carroll found that Asians had higher first-year persistence and second-year return rates than Whites (97 percent vs. 91 percent and 92 percent vs. 85 percent, respectively), but thereafter the rates for both were nearly identical. The only other difference occurred when only two-thirds of the remaining Asians returned for their fourth year of college compared to 80 percent of the Whites.

There are some differences in persistence rate between individual Asian groups. For instance, for the combined 1980–1982 freshman cohorts in the College of Letters and Science at the University of California, Berkeley, the overall five-year persistence rates for Filipinos (53 percent), "other Asians" (mostly Southeast Asians, 55 percent), and Koreans (63 percent) were lower than those for the remaining Asian groups (74 percent to 77 percent) as well as Whites (73 percent) (Frank, 1988). In each of the freshman cohorts from 1979 to 1982 at the University of Hawaii, Manoa, the first-year persistence rates of Native Hawaiians and Filipinos were usually lower (by 2 percent to 13 percent) than those for Japanese as well as for the total cohort (University of Hawaii, Department of Sociology, 1988).

*College Graduation Rate.* When viewed collectively, Asians tend to have graduation rates that are very much like those of Whites. Of the

1980 graduates in the High School and Beyond survey who entered post-secondary institutions by 1982, roughly one-third of both the Asians and the Whites had earned bachelor's degrees by 1986 (Eagle and others, 1988). In the 1981 and 1982 freshman cohorts at the University of Colorado, Boulder, both Asians and Whites had five-year graduation rates of approximately 50 percent (University of Colorado, 1987), and for the combined 1980-1982 freshman cohorts in the College of Letters and Science at the University of California, Berkeley, approximately two-thirds of both the Asians and Whites graduated in five years or less (Frank, 1988).

Data on the five-year graduation rates for the previously described freshman cohorts at the University of California, Berkeley, and the seven-year rates for the 1979 freshman cohort at the University of Hawaii, Manoa, suggest that the graduation rates for Filipinos, Southeast Asians, Native Hawaiians, and Koreans tend to be lower than those for other Asian groups as well as Whites (Frank, 1988; Takeuchi, Agbayani, and Kuniyoshi, 1988).

Like other students, Asians often take more than four years to complete work on their bachelor's degrees. For example, fewer than one-fourth of the Asian graduates in the 1979 freshman cohort at the University of Hawaii, Manoa, finished by their fourth year (and over 40 percent of the Native Hawaiians and Filipinos took six or seven years) (Takeuchi, Agbayani, and Kuniyoshi, 1988). Many factors contribute to this trend, including academic problems and enrollment in scientific and technical majors that take longer to finish. In addition, because of their financial need, some Asians will attend college on a part-time basis for long periods of time or "stop out" occasionally to earn income.

*Institutional Student Surveys.* Student surveys administered during and after the college years provide important data on perceptions of educational outcomes and the college environment and are frequently used to assess the impact of academic programs and to understand student development and experiences. Some illustrative examples of these types of data are presented below, primarily from surveys of the 1975 and 1981 freshman cohorts at the University of Colorado, Boulder (J. Endo, 1977, 1987; J. Endo and Bittner, 1985). Obviously, the extent to which these examples can be generalized to other institutions may be limited.

Asians, in the aggregate, tend to study in scientific and technical fields to a greater extent than Whites. Of the bachelor's degrees conferred on Asians nationally in 1984-85, nearly half were in such fields (18 percent were in the social sciences and 8 percent in the humanities), compared with 28 percent for Whites (Peng, 1988). Data on the academic majors of Asian students confirm this scientific and technical emphasis (see Peng, 1985; Sue and Abe, 1988), but there are differences between individual Asian groups (for instance, Filipinos and Native Hawaiians are less likely to be in these fields) and by nativity (native-born Asians are less likely to be in these fields) (see Chan, 1981; University of Hawaii, Department of Sociology, 1988; Frank, 1988).

It is therefore not surprising that at the University of Colorado, Asians more than Whites reported that it was important to learn about the physical and natural sciences, while Whites more than Asians said that it was important to learn about the social sciences and humanities. Further, Asians were more confident than Whites of their own quantitative skills and more apt to feel that their classes improved these skills. Outside their coursework, Asians were involved to a greater extent than Whites in science-related activities.

Asians at Colorado reported greater concerns than Whites over their reading, writing, and verbal skills. This was especially the case for recent immigrants and refugees. Among other consequences, such concerns made Asians less willing than Whites to participate in class discussions and often forced Asians to spend more time studying. However, compared with Whites, Asians felt it was less important to develop their communications skills and that their classes contributed less to the improvement of their writing abilities. In addition, Asian freshmen felt a greater need than Whites to enhance their time-management, test-taking, and study skills.

To a lesser extent than Whites, Asians at Colorado reported that their classes contributed to the development of the ability to integrate diverse material and of analytical skills to solve a variety of social, economic, political, and ethical problems. On the other hand, Asians felt more than Whites that their classes contributed to the development of critical-thinking skills and the ability to apply general concepts to new situations.

Asians were usually less satisfied than Whites with the quality of student-faculty interaction and had less confidence in their social skills, especially in relation to older adults. Asians reported engaging in discussions and seeking help on coursework and personal problems from peers rather than faculty and staff to a greater extent than Whites. Asians felt more than Whites that such problems greatly affected their ability to study.

Patterns of Asian involvement in extracurricular activities vary from institution to institution. Asians at Colorado were more active than Whites in high school activities like student government and subject-matter clubs but, in general, were less active than Whites in college and less satisfied with opportunities for engaging in extracurricular activities. A survey conducted for a Stanford University task force on minority issues found that Asians were more likely than Whites to participate in student government, ethnic cultural organizations and events, and service activities but were less apt to participate in intramural or intercollegiate athletics, campus media, fraternities and sororities, and religious activities (Stanford University, 1989).

For Asians as well as other minorities, academic, personal, and social development cannot be disassociated from the sense of support, acceptance, and belonging they receive from their institutional environment. At many colleges and universities, the nature of this environment has become problematic. For example, while Asians at the University of California, Berkeley, for the most part felt positive about their academic experiences in a recent study, they voiced serious concerns about their campus environment. They reported experiencing subtle racism, such as being left out of important activities, and they felt that faculty, staff, administrators, and other students were not sensitive to their needs. Immigrant students in particular faced academic and social problems, often because of their English-language skills, and had difficulty adjusting to campus life (University of California, Berkeley, 1989). In a study by a Stanford University task force on minority issues, about three-fourths of the Asians said they had experienced some form of discrimination or devaluation attributable to their ethnic background. A lower percentage of Asians than Whites felt that their overall experience at Stanford was rewarding. Asian students wanted more Asian faculty and counseling and advising staff who were sensitive to their backgrounds and needs, and they wanted Asian-American studies courses (Stanford University, 1989). Recent data showing that Berkeley and other selective institutions may be limiting the admission of Asian students reinforce Asian concerns about the quality of institutional environments (Wang, 1988; Nakanishi, 1988).

## Why Asians Perform the Way They Do on Assessment Measures

Most Asians place a very high value on formal education, including higher education. There are several reasons for this. Traditionally, education has been associated with status and respect in many Asian societies. The American-born descendants of the early Asian immigrants, particularly Chinese and Japanese, relied heavily on education for socioeconomic mobility, in part because other avenues were more restricted due to discrimination. Many achieved postwar mobility into the middle class, and they have continued the earlier pattern by instilling the value of education in their children. Recent Asian immigrants tend to be a fairly select population of ambitious individuals who, because of current immigration policies, often have good occupational skills and educational backgrounds. As parents, they are likely to push their children to seek higher education. Even immigrants from working-class backgrounds (and Southeast Asians refugees of diverse backgrounds) are highly motivated to take advantage of opportunities available in this country. This includes higher education for their children, which may be limited in their homelands to the wealthy or exceptionally talented. Finally, Asians, like other Americans, also realize that higher education provides the knowledge, skills, and credentials essential for good contemporary careers. For Asians, formal credentials and good jobs can be an important means for gaining social acceptance as well as economic security (Chan, 1981; Nishi, 1981).

Because of the high value placed on education, there are strong family, community, and peer pressures on most young Asians to study hard, get good grades, and earn a college degree. In addition, parents often sacrifice considerable time and energy to encourage and tutor their children. Asians in high school spend more time on homework, attend classes more regularly, take more academic courses, and have higher educational aspirations than Whites, according to data from the High School and Beyond survey (Peng, Owings, and Fetters, 1984). While in college, Asians continue to face pressures to succeed academically. These are a potential source of psychological problems, especially if the educational expectations of others cannot be met (Endo, 1980).

There are some overall differences between individual Asian groups in educational accomplishment. For instance, Filipino and Pacific Islander students tend to perform less well than many other Asians. This is particularly true for Filipinos and Pacific Islanders from Hawaii, where these groups are economically disadvantaged and face major social barriers. As a result, young Filipinos and Pacific Islanders may have comparatively low aspirations and poor basic skills, and because of inadequacies in the K-12 and higher education systems, they may not receive enough of the encouragement, preparation, financial resources, and other support necessary to attend and perform well in college (University of Hawaii, 1987; University of Hawaii, Department of Sociology, 1988; University of Hawaii, Task Force on Filipinos, 1988; Mau, 1987).

Unfortunately, little assessment data are available on Southeast Asians, who are now enrolling in college in increasing numbers. Southeast Asian students illustrate some of the differences in educational accomplishment between and within Asian groups. Research indicates that Vietnamese might generally be expected to perform better in higher education than Cambodians, Laotians, Hmong, and other refugees for reasons related to cultural values, family and community organization, parental socioeconomic and educational background, and experiences in the U.S. (see Rumbaut and Ima, 1988). In the case of the Hmong, there are major factors that work against their educational progress, such as patterns of early marriage and childbearing for girls, short-term economic aspirations, lack of role models and information networks, and limited financial resources (Rumbaut and Ima, 1988; Baizerman and Hendricks, 1988).

However, within all of the Southeast Asian groups, children who come to this country at a very young age and spend many years in American primary and secondary schools are more apt to do well in higher education than those who come at an older age. Youth who do not arrive with intact or functional families are more likely to be at-risk for educational difficulties. Also, youth who came after the "first wave" of refugees (after 1978) are more likely to have gone through very traumatic migration experiences and are less apt to have parents who are literate, have any knowledge of English, or have marketable occupational skills (see Rumbaut and Ima, 1988).

Similarly, among other (nonrefugee) Asians who are recent immigrants, there are differences in accomplishment in higher education due to socioeconomic background and length of residence and schooling in the U.S. In addition, both recent immigrant and refugee college students may experience problems because of financial need (many have to work long hours during the academic year) or because of family obligations and expectations. Immigrant and refugee students may further experience varying degrees of difficulty in adapting to the social environment of colleges and universities (especially if there are few Asian faculty, staff, support services, student groups, and courses) and may have to overcome feelings of alienation and isolation.

As discussed earlier, Asian college students tend to study in scientific and technical fields (particularly the physical sciences, computer science, and engineering) to a greater extent than Whites. Historically, these fields have been associated with modernity in many Asian countries and have been accorded high status. The American-born descendants of the early immigrants were encouraged to go into these fields, in part because of the tremendous expansion of these fields during the 1940s and 1950s. These pioneers served as role models for later generations, although native-born Asians now tend to go into these fields at a lower rate than recent immigrants.

New Asian immigrants and refugees are usually highly pragmatic about their economic circumstances. They often see the study of scientific and technical fields as providing marketable skills that will result in easily obtainable, well-paying, secure, high-status jobs. They believe they can do well in these fields despite English language deficiencies that might be a severe handicap in other areas. Many feel there is less discrimination in scientific and technical occupations and are aware of the large numbers of Asians who already have such jobs. Consequently, immigrant and refugee youth frequently aspire to careers in these areas and work especially hard to develop their mathematical and scientific abilities. These youth are usually heavily influenced by their parents and peers—and even by teachers and counselors who may "track" Asians into mathematics and science courses and curricula (Endo, 1980; Chan, 1981).

As noted previously, there are some differences between and within individual Asian groups in the level of interest in scientific and technical fields. In general, Filipinos and Pacific Islanders are generally less likely to study in these fields for several reasons, including a lack of role models and poorly developed quantitative skills. Also, native-born Asians tend to have more diverse career interests and expectations than the foreign-born and are less apt to be concentrated in scientific and technical fields.

Asians tend to do better on the math portions of standardized college admissions tests than on the verbal portions. To a large extent, this reflects the less well-developed English-language reading, writing, and verbal skills of some Asians, coupled with their much greater efforts to improve skills in mathematics and science in order to pursue college studies and careers in scientific and technical areas.

Problems with communication skills are related to the non-English language backgrounds of many Asian youth and their parents (major exceptions are households where the parents and children are native-born and Filipino and East Indian immigrants who come from societies where English is a primary medium of instruction). In addition, the cultural values of many Asian groups sometimes encourage fairly restrained behavior in the presence of authority figures like parents and teachers, which limits discussion and argument in family or classroom settings and does not promote the development of verbal abilities. Even in college, Asian students are often apprehensive about class participation, and they may bypass opportunities to improve their reading and writing skills by avoiding humanities and social science courses and majors and by fulfilling English requirements with less rigorous courses (Chan, 1985; Hsia, 1988).

## Recommendations

The preceding assessment data and discussion present a complex picture. On such assessment measures as college entrance tests, GPAs, and rates of participation, persistence, and graduation, Asians, when viewed collectively, appear to be doing relatively well in higher education. Unfortunately, this limited perspective masks significant problems and issues like the difficulties being experienced by many Pacific Islanders, Filipinos, Southeast Asians, and others that only become apparent when data are examined by individual Asian group. Also important are problems and issues that are revealed through other measures, such as students' perceptions of their educational outcomes and the college environment—for example, the concerns of Asian students about their own communications skills, their interaction with faculty, the pressures on them to achieve, racial insensitivity toward them, and the quality of their institutional environment.

Assessment programs and studies can help educators determine the educational progress of Asians. However, much of the current assessment-related data have limitations. The following bulleted items are recommendations for educators who intend to collect or use assessment data on Asians:

• Data should be collected in a manner that identifies the specific group background of each Asian respondent. Data analyses should present information by individual Asian group and make comparisons between groups (if not every group, at least those on campus that are the largest and those with the most significant educational problems). Assessment research that samples student respondents should oversample Asians in order to produce reliable findings.

• Data analyses should describe patterns of various characteristics within Asian groups. For instance, the distribution of test scores for certain groups may be bimodal, a fact that will not be apparent from means or medians. In addition, comparisons should be made between important subgroups; for example, between subgroups delineated by gender, nativity, generation, socioeconomic background, and level of English-language proficiency.

• Assessment programs and studies should include more measures of Asian social and personal development, for instance measures of social skills, self-concept, identity, self-reliance, and other factors that have relevance for educational progress.

• Assessment programs and studies should take into account the English-language proficiency of Asians, especially recent immigrants and refugees, and should not confuse difficulties in mastering English as a second language with the presence of language or learning disorders.

• To the extent that assessment processes rely on students' reading, writing, or verbal skills, or all of these, educators need to be aware of the problems some Asians have with these skills. Such assessment processes may not adequately measure the knowledge and abilities of Asian students that are not directly related to such skills. Assessment of all students could incorporate other evidence of learning, such as projects or portfolios.

• Assessment programs and studies should look at how well Asian students adjust to the social aspects of their institutional environment (for example, sense of acceptance or of alienation, degree of integration into campus social life, effects of subtle discrimination or the devaluing behaviors of others, management of cultural differences, and so on) and relate this to the more customary measures of educational performance.

• Some of the data in this chapter and other research (see Sue and Zane, 1985) suggest that Asian students make conscious trade-offs as part of their academic strategies to get through college. For example, in order to attain the good grades that are expected of them by their families and others, some Asians with relatively weak English-language skills may take mostly scientific and technical courses (rather than those that might be more appropriate for their needs, abilities, or interests), spend a considerable amount of time studying (to the exclusion of other activities), enroll for fewer credit hours, and suppress personal or social problems (and not seek help). Assessment programs and studies need to consider the trade-offs that students might make.

• Assessment programs and studies should be linked to the evaluation and development of specific academic and student-support programs. When the latter have little apparent impact or relevance for Asians, this should be examined in detail. For instance, Asians may be underrepresented in certain humanities and social science programs because of a lack of appropriate career counseling and writing-skills development activities (see Walsh College, 1988), or Asians may not seek help from traditional student-support programs because these do not have culturally sensitive services or personnel.

• Assessment programs and studies should look at the long-term career and other outcomes of education. For example, research shows that Asians, regardless of group or gender or nativity subgroup, do not get the same returns on their educational investments in terms of occupation and income as Whites (see Hsia, 1988; Cabezas and Kawaguchi, 1988).

• As assessment data on Asians are collected, analyzed, and reported from more institutions, the data need to be examined for overall national trends and broken down by type of institution, region, and other key variables.

• In general, more assessment data need to be collected and reported on Asians attending less selective institutions, those outside the West Coast, and community colleges. Also, more data are needed on Asian groups that seem to be the most at-risk for academic problems.

## Conclusion

While this chapter has focused on Asian and Pacific Americans, it has broad implications for all minority students. Most important, the performance on assessment measures by minority students of any background should be examined within an interpretive framework that is, to a certain degree, specific to that background. This framework should include an awareness of differences between (and within) specific groups that may compose a broad category like "Asian and Pacific Americans" and a knowledge of appropriate historical, cultural, and socioeconomic background elements. And, as is the case with Asian and Pacific Americans, the educational status of all minorities will be more comprehensively assessed by investigating characteristic academic and social needs and problems and by giving greater attention to such areas as social and personal development, adjustment processes, educational trade-offs, and long-term career outcomes.

## References

Baizerman, M., and Hendricks, G. *A Study of Southeast Asian Youth in the Twin Cities of Minneapolis and St. Paul, Minnesota.* Minneapolis: Southeast Asian Refugee Studies Project, University of Minnesota, 1988.

Cabezas, A., and Kawaguchi, G. "Empirical Evidence for Continuing Asian American Income Inequality: The Human Capital Model and Labor Market Segmentation." In G. Okihiro, S. Hune, A. Hansen, and J. Liu (eds.), *Reflections on Shattered Windows.* Pullman: Washington State University Press, 1988.

Carroll, C. "College Access and Persistence Among Asian Americans: Findings from the High School and Beyond Study." Paper presented at the annual meeting of the American Educational Research Association, New Orleans, La., April 1988.

Chan, S. *Contemporary Asian Immigration and Its Impact on Undergraduate Education at the University of California.* Berkeley: Center for Studies in Higher Education, University of California, 1981.

Chan, S. "They Shall Write!" Paper presented at the conference on Perspectives on Asian Standards in Higher Education, University of California, Santa Cruz, 1985.

Dodge, S. "SAT, ACT Scores Remain Steady or Drop Slightly." *Chronicle of Higher Education,* September 20, 1989, p. A37.

Eagle, E., Fitzgerald, R., Gifford, A., Zuma, J., and MPR Associates, Inc. *High School and Beyond: A Descriptive Summary of 1980 High School Sophomores: Six Years Later.* Washington, D.C.: National Center for Education Statistics, U.S. Department of Education, 1988.

Endo, J. "Characteristics of Asian American University Freshmen: A Comparison with Other Minorities and Whites." Paper presented at the annual meeting of the Western Conference of the Association for Asian Studies, Colorado Springs, Colo., October 1977.

Endo, J. Unpublished tabulations of data on the 1975 and 1981 freshmen cohorts in the Student Outcomes Model, University of Colorado, Boulder, 1987.

Endo, J. Unpublished tabulations of data on the 1988 Asian American freshman cohort, University of Colorado, Boulder, 1989.

Endo, J., and Bittner, T. "Developing and Using a Longitudinal Student Outcomes Data File: The University of Colorado Experience." In P. Ewell (ed.), *Assessing Educational Outcomes.* New Directions for Institutional Research, no. 47. San Francisco: Jossey-Bass, 1985.

Endo, R. "Asian Americans and Higher Education." *Phylon,* 1980, *51* (3), 367–378.

Frank, A. Data tables presented at the symposium on Access and Persistence Among Asian Americans: Reality, Policy and Theory at the annual meeting of the American Educational Research Association, New Orleans, La., April 1988.

Hsia, J. *Asian Americans in Higher Education and at Work.* Hillsdale, N.J.: Erlbaum, 1988.

Lujan, H. "Asian Pacific Americans and the Quality of Education: A Policy View." Paper presented at the annual meeting of the Association for Asian American Studies, Pullman, Wash., March 1988.

Mau, R. "College Aspirations and Alienation of Minority Groups: A Review of Four Studies." Paper presented at the annual conference of the National Association for Asian and Pacific American Education, Honolulu, Hawaii, April 1987.

Nakanishi, D. "Asian Pacific Americans and Selective Undergraduate Admissions." *Journal of College Admissions,* 1988, *118,* 17–26.

Nishi, S. "The Negative Implications of Misinterpreting the Educational Attainment Levels of Asian/Pacific Americans." Paper presented at the Asian Pacific American Research Seminars, National Association of Asian and Pacific American Education, 1981.

Olsen, L. *Crossing the Schoolhouse Border: Immigrant Students and the California Public Schools.* San Francisco: California Tomorrow, 1988.

Peng, S. "Enrollment Pattern of Asian American Students in Postsecondary Education." Paper presented at the annual meeting of the American Educational Research Association, Chicago, 1985.

Peng, S. "Attainment Status of Asian Americans in Higher Education." Paper presented at the annual conference of the National Association for Asian and Pacific Education, Denver, Colo., April 1988.

Peng, S., Owings, J., and Fetters, W. "School Experiences and Performance of Asian American High School Students." Paper presented at the annual meeting of the American Educational Research Association, New Orleans, La., 1984.

Ramist, L., and Arbeiter, S. *Unpublished Tabulations (of High School and College Performance by Race).* New York: College Entrance Examination Board, 1986.

Rumbaut, R., and Ima, K. *The Adaptation of Southeast Asian Refugee Youth: A Comparative Study.* San Diego, Calif.: Department of Sociology, San Diego State University, 1988.

Stanford University, Committee on Minority Issues. *Building a Multiracial, Multicultural University Community.* Stanford, Calif.: Stanford University, 1989.

Sue, S., and Abe, J. *Predictors of Academic Achievement Among Asian American and White Students.* New York: College Entrance Examination Board, 1988.

Sue, S., and Zane, N. "Academic Achievement and Socioemotional Adjustment Among Chinese University Students." *Journal of Counseling Psychology,* 1985, *32* (4), 570-579.

Suzuki, B. "Asian Americans in Higher Education: Impact of Changing Demographics and Other Social Forces." Paper presented at a national symposium on the Changing Demographics of Higher Education, The Ford Foundation, New York, 1988.

Takeuchi, D., Agbayani, A., and Kuniyoshi, L. "Higher Education in Hawaii: A Comparison of Graduation Rates Among Asian Americans and Native Hawaiians." Paper presented at the Cornell Symposium on Asian Americans and Higher Education, Cornell University, May 1988.

Turnbull, W. "Are They Learning Anything in College?" *Change,* 1985, *17* (6), 23-26.

U.S. Bureau of the Census. *1980 Census of Population: Asian and Pacific Islander Population in the United States: 1980.* Washington, D.C.: U.S. Government Printing Office, 1988.

University of California, Advisory Committee on Asian American Affairs. *Asian Americans at Berkeley.* Berkeley: University of California, 1989.

University of Colorado, Office of Research and Testing. *Minority Graduation and Persistence.* Boulder: University of Colorado, 1987.

University of Hawaii. *A Study to Improve Access to Public Higher Education Programs and Support Services for Minority Students: Report to the 1987 Legislature, SR 114, SD 1, 1986 Session.* Honolulu: University of Hawaii, 1987.

University of Hawaii, Department of Sociology and Social Science Research Institute. *Native Hawaiian Students at the University of Hawaii: Implications for Vocational and Higher Education.* Honolulu, Hawaii: Alu Like, 1988.

University of Hawaii, Task Force on Filipinos. *Pamantasan: Report of the University of Hawaii Task Force on Filipinos.* Honolulu: University of Hawaii, 1988.

Walsh College, Writing Across the Curriculum Program. *Writing Across the Curriculum: A Handbook for Participants.* Canton, Ohio: Walsh College, 1988.

Wang, L. "Meritocracy and Diversity in Higher Education: Discrimination Against Asian Americans in the Post-*Bakke* Era." *Urban Review,* 1988, *20* (3), 189–209.

*Jean J. Endo is assistant director in the office of institutional research at the University of Colorado, Boulder. She has designed and conducted research on academic marketing, attrition, student outcomes, and alumni.*

*This chapter addresses the nature of the research that is needed to confront the challenge of diversity. If research is to play a central role in assisting institutions, it must clarify the nature of questions to be addressed and the methodologies employed.*

# The Challenge of Diversity: Implications for Institutional Research

*Daryl G. Smith*

For years, the literature on higher education has contained many articles describing the changing demographics in American society, particularly the growing numbers of racial and ethnic minorities, and the implication of those changes for colleges and universities. And indeed, over the past two decades, American higher education has shown a clear evolutionary change in the composition of the student body.

In spite of this evolution, the tone of the literature is increasingly gloomy as assessments reveal the inadequacy of higher education in meeting the challenge of educating an increasingly diverse population of students. The racial and ethnic diversity of college enrollments that has resulted from past efforts and societal reforms is a hollow victory, however, for the following reasons:

• The college-going rate has declined for many racial and ethnic groups, particularly Latinos and Blacks.

• Ethnic groups are clustered in institutions with the least amounts of resources and prestige and are concentrated in a narrow range of fields that are in comparatively low demand. Black and Latino students are over-represented in the community colleges; research universities have few Black, Latino, or Native American students; and despite being well represented in research universities, certain Asian American groups are clustered in a narrow range of disciplines.

• The proportion of degree recipients that Black, Latino, and Native American students represent is dramatically below their proportion in classes of entering freshmen.

• Alienation, lack of involvement, marginalization, overt racism, and discrimination too often characterize the campus experience for minority students.

• The rewards of college education in terms of preparation for graduate and professional schools and career advancement for Blacks and Latinos lag behind those of Whites.

The American Council on Education's national report is one among many calling for dramatic new efforts. "America is moving backward, rather than forward, in its efforts to achieve the full participation of minority citizens" (Commission on Minority Participation, 1988). Indeed, the challenge of diversity is one of the most critical issues facing higher education today. Not only will successful involvement of diverse populations mark the difference between institutional survival and failure, and between educational quality and mediocrity, it will have significant social implications as well. The consequences of educational disenfranchisement of large populations cannot be ignored.

This chapter addresses the nature of the research that is needed to confront the challenge of diversity and the vital relationship of research to developing appropriate policies and program responses. While the focus of this chapter is on the role of institutional research, the issues extend to policy research in a context far broader than the academy.

## Framing the Questions

Both the concepts and the methods of institutional research have directed attention away from institutional factors associated with success, thereby restricting responses to the issues. The dominant focus has been on the student rather than the institution. If research is to play a central role in assisting institutions to address the demographic issues challenging them, then it must be sensitive to the complex questions inherent in institutional policies, practices, and environment. Research should be both formative and summative so that it can not only assess outcomes but also identify student and institutional factors associated with success.

The process of "naming" will be a significant element in the design of needed research. Edelman (1977) recognizes the importance of naming when he states that "how the problem is named involves alternative scenarios, each with its own facts, values, judgments and emotions" (p. 29). Naming is not simply an abstract concept—it is central to research. Jaramillo (1988) points out that when retention is named "the student dropout rate," it implies a problem with the student. Alternatively, when retention is named "institutional graduate rate," the focus is on the institution. Furthermore, Jaramillo says, "as long as we condone the use of metaphors which conjure up a scenario of individual initiative and responsibility for educational failure, change . . . will not occur" (p. 27). The definition of a problem can dramatically affect the types of solutions sought. This has particular implications for the education of minorities, where too often failure has been attributed to the student and the student's background. The field requires institutional research that focuses on institutional problems that inhibit minority success.

## Methodological Issues

The appropriate use of instruments and the validity of generalizing from existing data are two central methodological issues to be considered.

*Instrumentation.* As institutions are being challenged to demonstrate success and improve quality, the assessment movement has moved to the forefront of institutional research. Standardized tests are central to assessment because of their availability and sophistication and because they permit relatively objective comparisons among individuals, programs, and institutions. There is growing concern, however, that colleges and universities are not using these tests appropriately. Rather than their results being used to assist students, the tests are too often used as the sole criterion for selection, placement, and assessment, which has the effect of excluding minorities and women. There is also significant concern that these tests may not be the best predictors of minority-student outcomes.

The issue here is not simply that certain minority groups achieve lower average scores on the Scholastic Aptitude Test (SAT), for example, but rather that the predictive validity of the tests themselves is weak. There is evidence that there is a lower correlation between the SAT and first-year postsecondary school grades for Latinos and women than for Whites and males (Duran, 1986; Morris, 1981; Rendon and Nora, 1987; Verdugo, 1986). Recent court cases have ruled that exclusive reliance upon SAT and American College Test results in discrimination against women and minorities. The Educational Testing Service itself suggests that these instruments not be used as the sole source of information to decide on a student's academic abilities (*Fair Test Examiner,* 1989).

Multiple-choice standardized tests are only one form of assessment. Institutions are also beginning to use a variety of methods, including qualitative approaches. Many of these are designed to be used in developing formative, as well as summative, evaluations of institutional programs (Cross and Angelo, 1988; Gray, 1989; Kells, 1988; Pike, 1988; *Report of the Task Force . . . ,* 1989). Surveys, case studies, and interviews may be necessary to ensure that all factors related to student success are being considered. Whatever instruments are employed, institutions need to consider their methods carefully, particularly when differential performance based on class, race, and gender appears. Moreover, in light of continuing evidence about the lack of predictive validity of standardized tests, institutions need to be willing to ask whether using such tests simply preserves discrimination (Morris, 1981; Verdugo, 1986).

*Generalizability.* While researchers must necessarily cluster data in order to arrive at practical conclusions, generalizations too often cluster inappropriate groups. Just as language should be sensitive to how people wish to be described, the very process of classifying glosses over significant variations within groups. The U.S. Census Bureau, using the classification "Hispanic," groups together those of Mexican-American, Puerto Rican, Cuban, Central and South American origin (Brown, Rosen, and Hill, 1980); however, evidence shows that the experiences of these groups differ greatly, particularly in the context of higher education (Duran, 1986; Salganik and Maw, 1987).

The Asian American population is yet another important example of extreme internal diversity. The term Asian American includes over sixty different ethnic groups, ranging from Korean, Japanese, and Chinese to Cambodian and Vietnamese (Carter, Pearson, and Shavlik, 1988). The unfortunate tendency to assume that Asian Americans are a "model minority" ignores not only the wide variations between subgroups, but the issues of discrimination, access, and environmental pressure experienced by Asian Americans in general (Hsia, 1987, 1988; Sue, 1977).

## Conceptual Issues

While the role of student characteristics continues to be important, increasing attention must be focused on the institutional climate and the degree to which it inhibits or fosters academic achievement.

*Student Characteristics.* The classic literature assessing student experiences, persistence, and performance in institutions of higher learning concludes that background characteristics including high school grades, socioeconomic status, academic aptitude, and parental education are among the strongest predictors of student persistence and college grade-point average (Astin, 1975; Cope and Hannah, 1975; Pantages and Creedon, 1978). Although these variables have often been the best predictors of persistence in school, they still account for only 10-to-12 percent of the variance. In other words, academic background, even for traditional students, has not been a very potent explanation of attrition (Astin, 1982; Tinto, 1987) or grades (Astin, 1982; Nettles, 1988).

The existing research on the factors associated with the academic success of minority populations is now growing. The results suggest that while academic preparation factors continue to be important, attitudinal and other variables are also very significant (Arciniega, 1985; Astin, 1982; Bennett and Okinaka, 1984; Burrell, 1980; Fields, 1988; Nettles, 1988). Sedlacek (1982) and Tracey and Sedlacek (1984) compared Black and White students, concluding that noncognitive factors such as self-confidence, understanding of racism, and community involvement are more significant than academic ability in predicting persistence. Suen (1983) found that dropout rates for Whites related to academic variables, but such rates for Blacks were related more to measures of social estrangement. Nor does academic preparation explain the high dropout rates for Latinos (Tinto, 1987). And Nora (1988), in an elegant study of Latinos in six community colleges, found that commitment to the institution and to educational goals were important indicators of retention. External factors such as work and family demands play significant roles for Chicanas (Chacon, Cohen, and Strover, 1986; Zambrana, 1987). Language skills and generational status may also be potentially important (Duran, 1986). Clearly, institutional research on student characteristics must be broad enough to tap the multiple sets of individual characteristics that affect success and the variations within and between subgroups.

*Institutional Responses to Student Needs.* Studies of institutions with the best records of success in admitting and retaining minority students reflect striking similarities. Many focus on the need to create strong programs that attempt to facilitate academic and social integration. These efforts include the following:

- Providing students with the tools to succeed through academic support, financial assistance, intensive advising, and the evaluation and monitoring of student progress (Cardoza, 1986; Blake, 1987)
- Developing increased coordination with elementary and secondary schools and community colleges (*A Difference of Degrees . . .* , 1987)
- Creating an accepting campus climate, or an "academic environment that nourishes and encourages students to succeed" (Commission on Minority Participation . . . , 1988)
- Developing access to adequate information and good data bases on groups of students, the barriers they face, and the factors associated with their successful completion of their programs
- Providing strong and focused leadership.

*Institutional Climate.* A common denominator of successful institutions—whether they are predominantly White or minority—is their focus on students' success and presumed capacity for success. This focus creates a more benign environment in which individuals can learn with encouragement and without harmful race or gender-based assumptions. The underlying theme in this research is the importance of the attitudes and climate of the institution, quite apart from specific program responses.

While creating a positive climate is often recommended, this is perhaps the most challenging goal. Campus climates are becoming increasingly volatile, including incidents of racist attacks and efforts to denigrate minorities.

The following quote by Bornholdt (1987, pp. 6–7) speaks about her concern for the climate of American higher education:

> If a Rip Van Winkle who retired in 1966 came back today, resumed his reading of the *Chronicle of Higher Education* and browsed through . . . *Change*, he would have to wonder not at the magnitude of change since 1965, but at the continuity of problems. . . . The statistics for Blacks are anything but cheering. . . . Yet perhaps the most conspicuous change a Rip would note is the deteriorated climate for interracial unity. . . . The presence of Blacks in higher education falls woefully short of where men and women of good will hoped and trusted it would be by 1987.

The literature concerning the campus environment for Black students is reasonably substantial (Allen, 1982, 1988; Morris, 1979; Nettles, 1986; Peterson and others, 1978; Loo and Rolison, 1986; Patterson and Sedlacek, 1984). Literature is growing on Latinos, emerging on Asians, and scarce on Native Americans (Chacon, Cohen, and Strover, 1986; Hsia, 1988; Olivas, 1986; Oliver, 1985; Sanders, 1987; Suen, 1983; Sue, 1981; Webster, 1984). In all cases, the conclusions are inescapable—the climate for minorities on campus is more alienating than involving. On more and more campuses racism and racial hostility are no longer thinly disguised. Sadly, on many campuses racism is a fact of life.

Crosson concurs: "While the scope and depth of racist and discriminatory attitudes and behavior are unknown, it is clear that many predominantly white four year colleges and universities have somehow failed to live up to their ideals as civil and tolerant social communities that respect diversity and pluralism" (Crosson, 1988, p. 381).

*Fundamental Transformation: Organizing the Institution for Diversity.* Higher education must once again rethink what it does and how. At the core of this effort will be the improved capacity of the organization to educate in a pluralistic society for a pluralistic world. Looking only to individuals for predictors of success cannot work well enough or fast enough. In addition to whether students are prepared for learning, a serious question for researchers is whether institutions are prepared for diversity.

The traditional input-process-outcomes model of assessment in higher education assumes that student characteristics interact with those of the institution. Higher-education research literature does not ignore the institution, but it does emphasize student characteristics as the important elements in student performance. There are a number of logical reasons for this focus. First, many studies deal only with one institution, so that institutional characteristics are constant while student characteristics and student performance vary. Second, multi-institutional studies place heavy emphasis on the structural characteristics of the institution. Most institutions cannot change these factors. Third, the natural assumption has been that because student-institution "fit" is important, students who are successful in particular types of institutions need to be identified. Institutions historically have shown more desire to select who comes to the institution than willingness to change the institution itself. Thus, despite a model that suggests that individuals and institutions interact to affect outcomes, the focus of many studies has been on student characteristics, particularly academic preparation.

Focusing on the preparation needs of minority students will continue to be an important institutional priority. However, many institutions are also recognizing significant institutional barriers to the success of minority students. Unless the issue is addressed at this level, programs run the risk of simply helping students adjust, manage, and survive in an alien environment where they never become comfortable. In light of the critical importance of student involvement in education and the growing racial crisis on many campuses, research on access and performance must be expanded to the institution itself, the attitudes and values of the community, and the education of all students and all members of the community. In this context, institutions need to assess their mission, their climate, and the ability of all members of the community—students, staff, faculty, and governing boards—to function in a pluralistic environment.

## Questions and Implications for Assessment

On many campuses, the challenge of pluralistic transformation requires grappling with a number of complex issues that influence the role of institutional research and assessment. An assessment program that attends to the institution and community, as well as to students, will become an important element in efforts to reform. A number of general measures of institutional performance, student satisfaction, and student involvement are available through the American College Testing service, the Educational Testing Service, the National Center for Higher Education Management Systems, and the University of California, Los Angeles. Specific institutional approaches to assessing the campus climate for diversity, such as Stanford's "Building a Multiracial, Multicultural University Community," can also be very helpful. Regardless of the specific approaches, the institution's assessment process must be designed to incorporate as many diverse perspectives as possible. Although assessment is too new to offer prescribed methods, what follows is a discussion of some of the complex issues and questions that need to be addressed as part of an assessment effort.

*Key Issue: Student Success.* Four common student-centered approaches can assess the success of institutions in organizing for diversity: the numbers and percentages of racial and ethnic minorities in the student body, retention and graduation rates of students, satisfaction of students with the educational experience, and performance measures such as grades, test results, courses taken, and behavioral measures. Each of these provides a foundation for assessment efforts. Each approach requires attention to group and gender differences and similarities. Research suggests that while the presence of a certain number of minority students will not in and of itself create a hospitable climate for diversity, a "critical mass" of such students may be essential to avoid some of the inevitable consequences of tokenism and isolation (Kanter, 1977). In interpreting results from student success data, the focus should be on the organizational factors that have affected success in each domain.

Relevant research questions for institutional assessment include the following:

• What is the demographic makeup of the student body?
• How has this changed over the last ten years?
• How is it changing now?
• What are the retention and graduation rates among all student groups?
• What is the satisfaction of students overall and within student groups?
• What feedback do alumni have about their experiences?
• What factors in the institution and student body promote student success?
• What special initiatives is the institution pursuing, and what effects are they having on minority students' experiences and success?

*Key Issue: Diversity of Faculty and Staff.* One of the most significant reasons to increase diversity of faculty and staff lies beyond the obvious need for role models for students. In institutions that are organizing for diversity, multiple perspectives are essential at all levels of decision-making and program development because no single individual or group of individuals can begin to represent the variety required. However, the challenge of establishing such diversity in faculty and staff is complex. The inadequacy of the minority "pipeline" is one of the most critical factors challenging successful diversification of key personnel in higher education (Blackwell, 1988). However, just as retention and development of students have become as critical as student access, we now need to focus on the fact that retention and development of faculty and staff must become as important as availability.

Relevant research questions include the following:

• What is the diversity pattern of the faculty and staff?
• Are minority individuals clustered in special programs and fields?
• What roles are minorities playing in decision-making at the student, program, and institutional level?
• What is their level of satisfaction and retention?
• What efforts are being made for their professional development?
• To what degree are they isolated from the mainstream activities of the institution?
• Do they feel marginalized?

*Key Issue: Quality of Interaction Between Members of the Community and Between Students and the Academic Program.* Research evidence reflects the importance of student involvement with the institution. Positive interaction between peers and between students and faculty and student involvement with the curriculum and academic program are key elements in student retention and performance. However, we do not know much about the nature of these dynamics for minorities. Some researchers have found evidence of a direct role for student involvement in predicting student success; others have found significant racial and gender differences in the kinds of involvement that are important; and others have found evidence only for an indirect role for measures of involvement (Crosson, 1988; Nettles, 1988; Pascarella, 1985; Tinto, 1987). Nevertheless, the institutional involvement theme is pervasive enough that it must be taken seriously. Here again, the focus must move beyond the actions of students to the institutional qualities and structures that invite involvement. The research questions in this area deal with the quality of interaction; attitudes of faculty, staff, and students; perceptions of institutional values; and the campus climate.

Relevant research questions include the following:

- To what degree are students of different racial and ethnic groups involved in the life of the institution?
- What roles do different kinds of involvement (social, academic, peer, faculty) play in student performance and persistence?
- What are the attitudes on campus toward interracial relations and contact?
- Do students feel that the institution values diversity and supports these goals?
- Do members of the community support goals for diversity?
- Have policies been scrutinized and enforced in an effort to include, not exclude?
- Are inappropriate behaviors dealt with decisively?
- What is the general climate on campus?

*Key Issue: Mission and Values.* Values issues affect pluralism in many ways. Perhaps the greatest challenge occurs when students perceive that their values and perspectives are not appreciated and may even conflict with institutional norms and behaviors. At worst, students may perceive that they must abandon their own cultural values and adopt other prevailing values in order to succeed (Ogbu, 1978). Cooperation versus competition and individual versus community have been described as two such value domains where preferred modes of relating and learning may conflict with dominant institutional values. If an individual or group prefers cooperative relationships and learning in an institution that stresses individualism and competition, it creates a fundamental tension that can seriously impede the learning process. Grading on a curve, where the success of some students works to the disadvantage of others, is an example of an institutionally valued device that conflicts with the cultural perspective or preferred learning style of some students.

Institutions need to be very clear in differentiating between values that facilitate learning and values that marginalize some groups. At the same time, institutions need to be open to new ways of accomplishing goals. Evidence suggests the benefits of cooperative learning and the potential harm of competition (Astin, 1987; Palmer, 1987). Competitive environments may actually be detrimental to all students, not just a particular group.

Relevant research questions include the following:

• Does the institution communicate values that are at odds with the cultures and communities of racial and ethnic minorities?
• Do some explicit or implicit values alienate, rather than involve, particular groups?
• How does the campus express its goals and values?

*Key Issue: Educating for Diversity.* More and more institutions are beginning to articulate a commitment to educate all students for a pluralistic world and to create environments that can embrace diversity. The content of the curriculum, styles of teaching, and modes of assessment are all potential means to enhance these goals.

Relevant research questions include the following:

• To what degree are students aware of diversity in their institution, state, and country?
• How knowledgeable are students about ethnic diversity and the histories and cultures of those from whom they differ?
• To what degree does the curriculum reflect new scholarship dealing with race, cultural pluralism, and learning?
• How does the institution accommodate varieties of learning styles?
• What efforts are being made to involve all faculty and staff in the creation of new curricular and pedagogical approaches?

*Key Issue: Dealing with Conflict.* Even the most superficial analysis of many college campuses suggests that conflict is either openly present or just under the surface. Some degree of conflict is expected when individuals and groups from diverse backgrounds come together in an institutional setting (Jones, 1987). Increased numbers of peers may make a setting more comfortable for minority group members, but may threaten the majority. This dynamic can intensify conflict as campuses become more diverse or more explicit in their commitment to diversity.

The classic literature on intergroup relations suggests, moreover, that certain common conditions increase conflict: a competitive environment, unequal status of individuals and groups, frustration caused by hostile environments, perceptions of unresponsiveness by some and favoritism by others, and little focus for meaningful contact between groups (Amir, 1969). Yet symptoms of conflict may indicate that the institution is grappling with such issues and is in the process of fundamental change. Indeed, an ongoing study of ten "successful" institutions suggests that conflict may be necessary to assist institutions in identifying which changes are essential. Therefore, conflict can be a pathway to learning (Green, 1989; Richardson, Simmons, and de los Santos, 1987; Skinner and Richardson, 1988).

Relevant research questions follow:

- What is the level of conflict on campus?
- How is the institution dealing with differences between people?
- Are differences valued or viewed as negative?
- How adequate is communication at all levels of the institution?

*Key Issue: Perceived Conflict Between Diversity and Quality.* A continuing message that open access for minorities to an academic institution fundamentally conflicts with student quality is perhaps the most disturbing sign of inadequate institutional approaches to diversity (Birnbaum, 1988; Skinner and Richardson, 1988). Given the national focus on effectiveness, this apparent conflict must be addressed.

Concern about lowering admission standards comprises much of the discussion about improving institutional quality. There is reason to believe that this concern and its underlying assumptions lead to an inappropriate conflict between quality and access. There are several important points to be made:

- The concern about preparation of students for higher education is *not* one regarding minorities, although it affects many minority students. While the impact on those who come from disadvantaged backgrounds is more devastating, the declining preparation of students is a national issue affecting virtually all schools and all students.

- Admissions policies of institutions of higher education have always reflected different levels of preparation between students. Even the most highly selective institutions have sought geographic, athletic, artistic, and leadership diversity among their students rather than populations of perfect grades and SAT scores. Until recently, there has been little question that quality and diversity are complementary; quality was presumed to embrace the contributions of those with different strengths. Moreover, there has been widespread recognition that grades and test scores could not encompass all that is needed for success.

• Much of the evidence concerning the tension between quality and diversity rests on the lower average scores of minorities on standardized tests. Yet, as indicated elsewhere, the predictive validity and power of these instruments are by no means established and are often poor, especially for women and minorities. The same could be said for learning assessment programs that rely on these kinds of measures. Using multiple, diverse achievement indicators has been proven to be preferable for purposes of adequate assessment and does not require lowering standards for learning. Indeed, one of the characteristics of successful institutions is that they set high standards and expectations and support students' efforts to achieve them. Arturo Madrid (1988) has suggested that measuring quality using only one method creates conflict between quality and diversity. The implication is that we can broaden our understanding and definition about quality without diluting expectations for learning or the curriculum.

The fundamental predisposition of higher education has been to maintain homogeneity and to adapt only when necessary (Morris, 1981; Verdugo, 1986). Current discussions about institutions setting limits on access for Asian Americans are a critical example (Hsia, 1987; Jaschik, 1987). The credibility of an institution's commitment to diversity and quality is weakened when it limits access by Asian Americans in the name of diversity and by Black and Latino students in the name of quality. The net result of both is to perpetuate homogeneity.

Relevant research questions regarding quality and diversity may include the following:

• How does the institution use standardized tests?
• Is there an explicit or underlying assumption that diversity and quality are at odds?
• What measures of performance and success could minimize problems of bias?
• How are issues of quality and diversity reflected in the hiring and promotion of faculty and staff?
• What are the expectations for success in the environment?

## Conclusion

What will institutions committed to pluralism look like? We do not yet know the answer to this question. The challenge of diversity has been part of the social agenda since this country's founding. It will be an increasingly important element of the dialogue that must occur in higher education in the years to come. Creating pluralistic communities will involve fundamental change and will require a greater capacity to deal with conflict. Bringing together diverse people in a common enterprise requires not just the reconciliation of differences but an appreciation of them. The focus of attention, assessment, and change must include the entire institutional community, not just particular student groups.

An institution that organizes for diversity will derive many benefits, not the least of which will be the increased capacity to respond to change (Weick, 1979). There will also be opportunities for

- Curricular revitalization
- New approaches to policy and organization
- The development and growth of "global villages" on campuses
- Dialogue concerning conditions that foster good teaching and learning
- Environments that appreciate racial, cultural, and ethnic differences
- Development of a consensus on essential values for the academic mission and the creation of a sense of community
- Benefits from diverse teaching approaches
- The excitement of learning in a cross-cultural climate.

Clarifying the questions we ask, the data we collect, and the conclusions we draw is a critical role for research in this time of change. The challenge of diversity is not primarily the deficits of minorities; it is an opportunity to improve the quality of our institutions and their capacity to change.

## References

Allen, W. *Undergraduate Survey of Black Undergraduate Students Attending Predominantly White, State Supported Universities.* Ann Arbor: Center for Afro American and African Studies, Michigan University, 1982. (ED 252 615)

Allen, W. "The Education of Black Students on White College Campuses: What Quality the Experience." In M. T. Nettles (ed.), *Toward Black Undergraduate Student Equality in American Higher Education.* Westport, Conn.: Greenwood Press, 1988.

Amir, Y. "Contact Hypotheses in Ethnic Relations." *Psychological Bulletin,* 1988, 71 (5), 314-342.

Arciniega, T. *Hispanics and Higher Education: A CSU Imperative.* Long Beach: Office of the Chancellor, California State University, 1985.

Astin, A. W. *Preventing Students from Dropping Out: A Longitudinal, Multi Institutional Study of College Dropouts.* San Francisco: Jossey-Bass, 1975.

Astin, A. W. *Minorities in American Higher Education: Recent Trends, Current Prospects, and Recommendations.* San Francisco: Jossey-Bass, 1982.

Astin, A. W. "Competition or Cooperation." *Change,* 1987, 19 (5), 12-19.

Bennett, C., and Okinaka, A. "Explanations of Black Student Attrition in Predominantly White and Predominantly Black Universities." *Integrated Education,* 1984, 22 (13), 73-80.

Birnbaum, R. "Administrative Commitments and Minority Enrollments." *Review of Higher Education,* 1988, 11 (4), 435-458.

Blackwell, J. "Faculty Issues: The Impact of Minorities." *Review of Higher Education,* 1988, 11 (4), 417-434.

66    THE EFFECT OF ASSESSMENT ON MINORITY STUDENT PARTICIPATION

Blake, E. "Equality for Blacks." *Change,* 1987, *19* (3), 10-13.
Bornholdt, L. "Time for a Second Generation Effort." *Change,* 1987, *19* (3), 6-7.
Brown, G. H., Rosen, N. L., and Hill, S. T. *The Condition of Education for Hispanic Americans.* Washington, D.C.: National Center for Educational Statistics, 1980.
Burrell, L. F. "Is There a Future for Black Students on Predominantly White Campuses?" *Integrated Education,* 1980, *18* (5-6), 23-27.
Cardoza, J. "Colleges Alerted: Pay Attention to Minorities or Risk Future Survival." *ETS Development,* 1986, *32* (3), 8-10.
Carter, D., Pearson, C., and Shavlik, D. "Double Jeopardy: Women of Color in Higher Education." *Educational Record,* 1988, *69* (1), 86-103.
Chacon, M., Cohen, E., and Strover, S. "Chicanas and Chicanos: Barriers to Progress." In M. A. Olivas (ed.), *Latino College Students.* New York: Teachers College Press, 1986.
Commission on Minority Participation in Education and American Life. *One-Third of a Nation.* Washington, D.C.: American Council on Education, 1988.
Cope, R., and Hannah, W. *Revolving Door Colleges: The Causes and Consequences of Dropping Out, Stopping Out, and Transferring.* New York: Wiley, 1975.
Cross, P., and Angelo, T. *Classroom Assessment Techniques.* Ann Arbor, Mich.: National Center for Research to Improve Teaching and Learning, 1988.
Crosson, P. "Four Year College and University Environments for Minority Degree Achievement." *Review of Higher Education,* 1988, *11* (4), 365-382.
*A Difference of Degrees: State Initiative to Improve Minority Student Achievement Research Report.* Denver, Colo.: State Higher Education Executive Officers, 1987.
Duran, R. "Prediction of Hispanics' College Achievement." In M. A. Olivas (ed.), *Latino College Students.* New York: Teachers College Press, 1986.
Edelman, J. *Political Language: Words That Succeed and Policies That Fail.* New York: Academic Press, 1977.
*Fair Test Examiner,* 1989, *3* (entire issue 2).
Fields, C. "The Hispanic Pipeline: Narrow, Leaking and Needing Repair." *Change,* 1988, *20* (3), 20-27.
Gray, P. J. *Achieving Assessment Goals Using Evaluation Techniques.* New Directions for Higher Education, no. 67. San Francisco: Jossey-Bass, 1989.
Green, M. *Minorities on Campus: A Handbook for Enhancing Diversity.* Washington, D.C.: American Council on Education, 1989.
Hsia, J. *Asian American Students: Ability, Achievement and Access to Higher Education.* Paper presented at the meeting of the American Educational Research Association, Washington, D.C., April 1987.
Hsia, J. "Asian Americans Fight the Myth of the Super Student." *Educational Record,* 1988, *68* (4), 94-97.
Jaramillo, M. "Institutional Responsibility in the Provision of Educational Experiences to the Hispanic American Female Student." In T. McKenna and F. I. Ortiz (eds.), *The Broken Web.* Encino, Calif.: Floricant Press, 1988.
Jaschik, S. "350 Asian American Leaders Create Statewide Lobbying Group to Influence the Policies of Higher Education in California." *Chronicle of Higher Education,* November 25, 1987, pp. A21, A24.
Jones, W. T. "Enhancing Minority-White Peer Interactions." In D. J. Wright (ed.), *Responding to the Needs of Today's Minority Students.* New Directions for Student Services, no. 38. San Francisco: Jossey-Bass, 1987.
Kanter, R. M. *Men and Women of the Corporation.* New York: Basic Books, 1977.
Kells, H. R. *Self Study Processes.* New York: American Council on Education, 1988.

Loo, C., and Rolison, G. "Alienation of Ethnic Minority Students at a Predominantly White University." *Journal of Higher Education*, 1986, 57 (1), 59-77.

Morris, L. *Elusive Equality*. Washington, D.C.: Howard University, 1979.

Morris, L. "The Role of Testing in Institutional Selectivity and Black Access to Higher Education." In G. E. Thomas (ed.), *Black Access to Higher Education*. Westport, Conn.: Greenwood Press, 1981.

Nettles, M. T. "Black and White Students' College Performance in Majority White and Majority Black College Settings." In J. B. Williams (ed.), *Title VI Regulations for Higher Education: Problems and Progress*. New York: Teachers College Press, 1986.

Nettles, M. T. *Toward Black Undergraduate Student Equality in American Higher Education*. Westport, Conn.: Greenwood Press, 1988.

Nora, A. "Determinants of Retention Among Chicano College Students: A Structural Model." *Research in Higher Education*, 1988, 26 (1), 31-57.

Ogbu, J. *Minority Education and Caste: The American System in Cross Cultural Perspective*. New York: Academic Press, 1978.

Olivas, M. A. (ed.). *Latino College Students*. New York: Teachers College Press, 1986.

Oliver, M. "Brown and Black in White: The Social Adjustment and Academic Performance of Chicano and Black Students in a Predominantly White University." *Urban Review*, 1985, 17 (1), 3-23.

Palmer, P. "Community Conflict and Ways of Knowing." *Change*, 1987, 19 (5), 20-25.

Pantages, T., and Creedon, C. "Studies of College Attrition: 1950-1975." *Review of Educational Research*, 1978, 48 (1), 49-101.

Pascarella, E. "Racial Differences in Factors Associated with Bachelor's Degree Completion: A Nine Year Follow Up." *Research in Higher Education*, 1985, 23 (4), 351-373.

Patterson, A., and Sedlacek, W. "Differences Among Minority Student Backgrounds and Attitudes Toward a University and Its Services." *Integrated Education*, 1984, 22, 95-101.

Peterson, M. W., Blackburn, R. T., Garrison, R., Arce, J., Davenport, T., and Mingle, M. *Black Students on White Campuses*. Ann Arbor, Mich.: Institute for Social Research, 1978.

Pike, G. "Review of Assessment Instruments." In C. Adelman (ed.), *Performance Judgment: Essays on Principles and Practices in the Assessment of College Student Learning*. Washington, D.C.: U.S. Government Printing Office, 1988.

Rendon, L., and Nora, A. *Hispanics in the Educational Pipeline*. Paper presented at a meeting of RAZA Advocates for California Higher Education, Irvine, California, October 1987.

*Report of the Task Force on Post Secondary Quality Assessment*. St. Paul: Minnesota Higher Education Coordinating Board, January 1989.

Richardson, R. C., Simmons, H., and de los Santos, A. G. "Graduating Minority Students." *Change*, 1987, 19 (3), 20-27.

Salganik, L., and Maw, C. *Factors Affecting Hispanics' Participation and Persistence in Postsecondary Education*. Paper presented at the annual meeting of the American Educational Research Association, Washington, D.C., April 1987.

Sanders, D. "Cultural Conflicts: An Important Factor in the Academic Failures of American Indian Students." *Journal of Multicultural Counseling and Development*, 1987, 15 (2), 81-90.

Sedlacek, W. *The Validity and Reliability of a Noncognitive Measure of Nonstudent Retention* (Research Report No. 3-82). College Park: University of Maryland, 1982.

Skinner, E., and Richardson, R. *Resolving Access, Quality Tensions, Minority Participation and Achievement in Higher Education.* Paper presented at the Association for the Study of Higher Education, St. Louis, Mo., November 1988.

Sue, D. "Counselling the Culturally Different." *Personnel and Guidance Journal,* 1977, *55* (7), 422-425.

Sue, D. *Counselling the Culturally Different.* New York: Wiley, 1981.

Suen, H. "Alienation and Attrition of Black Students on a Predominantly White Campus." *Journal of College Student Personnel,* 1983, *24* (2), 117-121.

Tinto, V. *Leaving College.* Chicago: University of Chicago Press, 1987.

Tracey, T., and Sedlacek, W. "Noncognitive Variables in Predicting Academic Success by Race." *Measurement and Evaluation in Guidance,* 1984, *16,* 171-178.

Verdugo, R. "Educational Stratification and Hispanics." In M. A. Olivas (ed.), *Latino College Students.* New York: Teachers College Press, 1986.

Webster, D. S. "Chicano Students in American Higher Education." *Integrated Education,* 1984, *22* (1), 42-51.

Zambrana, R. "A Profile of Chicana Women in Higher Education: Institutional Barriers." Working paper. University of California, Los Angeles, 1987.

*Daryl G. Smith is associate professor of education and psychology at the Claremont Graduate School, Claremont, California.*

*Montclair State College is typical of many smaller public campuses that must respond to state mandates for student outcomes assessment. Montclair's experience suggests lessons for others to ensure fairness for minority students.*

# Assessing Program Effectiveness in an Institution with a Diverse Student Body

*Mildred Garcia*

Educational institutions across the country are being urged or forced to assess programs as part of public insistence on their accountability for the academic success of their students. The state colleges, whose missions include ethnic diversity, are not exempted and in fact are primary targets of the assessment movement. This chapter examines the issues of assessment and diversity at state colleges by reviewing how one state college is dealing with assessment and minority participation.

## Institutional Profile

Montclair State College is one of nine state colleges located in northern New Jersey. It offers forty-four undergraduate majors, twenty-seven graduate majors, and numerous interdisciplinary programs, minors, and concentrations in five schools: Business Administration, Fine and Performing Arts, Humanities and Social Sciences, Mathematical and Natural Sciences, and Professional studies. In the fall of 1987, the undergraduate population of 10,135 included 2,651 undeclared majors, 26.2 percent of the total. The remaining students were distributed between the five schools as follows: Business Administration—2,094 students (20.7 percent); Fine and Performing Arts—831 students (8.2 percent); Mathematical and Natural Sciences—791 students (7.8 percent); Humanities and Social Sciences—2,421 students (23.9 percent); and Professional Studies—1,347 students (13.3 percent).

New Directions for Institutional Research, no. 65, Spring 1990 © Jossey-Bass Inc., Publishers

The student population comes primarily from Essex, Bergen, Passaic, Morris, and Hudson counties. The undergraduate population is White (80.1 percent), Latino (9 percent), Black (7.9 percent), and other races (3 percent), and mainly female (63.4 percent). Students are admitted into the college in a variety of ways. The regular admissions program, not unlike that of other state colleges, requires students to have a high school diploma or its equivalent and sixteen high school subject units that include English, social studies, mathematics, science, a foreign language, and electives. In addition there are three special admissions programs: the Educational Opportunity Fund (EOF), the Special Tutorial Program (STP), and the Special Talent Program.

## The Entering Class of 1987

The college enrolled 2,627 undergraduate students in the fall of 1987, of which 1,811 (69 percent) attended full-time and 816 (31 percent) attended part-time. The largest percent (37.7 percent) enrolled as regular full-time freshmen. The remainder of the full-time students consisted of 17.6 percent transfer students, 10.8 percent special admissions, 1.8 percent weekend college students, and 1.1 percent nonclassified students.

The part-time cohort consisted of 14.2 percent freshmen students, 9 percent transfer students, 7.6 percent nonclassified students, and 0.2 percent weekend college students.

*Ethnic Distribution.* Of the total entering class of 1987, 75.8 percent were White, 8.8 percent Black, 7.4 percent Latino, 2.7 percent Asian or Pacific Islanders, 0.06 percent American Indian, and 4.2 percent did not identify their ethnicity. The ethnic distribution of the population and the way they were admitted into the college are shown in Table 1. The majority of the White (64 percent) and Asian and Pacific Islander (54.8 percent) populations were admitted as regular full-time and part-time freshmen. In contrast, both the Black population and the Latino population were admitted mainly through the special admissions program, 66.2 percent and 61.4 percent, respectively.

*High School Class Rank.* High school class ranks for those students who entered through the regular admissions program ranged from 20 to 100 with the mean at the 78th percentile. Half (50.1 percent) were clustered in the 80-to-99th percentile, 41.6 percent in the 60-to-79th percentile, 8 percent in the 40-to-59th percentile, and 0.3 percent in the 20-to-39th percentile.

The students who entered through the special admissions program fell within the 0-to-100 range of high school class ranks with a mean at the 58th percentile. About one-fifth (21.6 percent) clustered in the 80-to-99th percentile, 24.6 percent in the 60-to-79th percentile, 26.5 percent in the 40-to-59th percentile, 16.4 percent in the 20-to-39th percentile, and

## Table 1.  Ethnic Distribution of Entering Class,
## Montclair State College, 1987

| Admission Studies | Whites (No.) | (%) | Asian / Pacific Islanders (No.) | (%) | Blacks (No.) | (%) | Latinos (No.) | (%) |
|---|---|---|---|---|---|---|---|---|
| Regular full-time freshmen | 901 | 49.7 | 23 | 36.0 | 28 | 13.3 | 32 | 18.1 |
| Part-time freshmen | 259 | 14.3 | 12 | 18.8 | 20 | 9.5 | 15 | 8.5 |
| Full-time transfer | 405 | 22.4 | 14 | 21.8 | 14 | 6.7 | 14 | 8.0 |
| Part-time transfer | 187 | 10.3 | 4 | 6.2 | 9 | 4.3 | 7 | 4.0 |
| Special admissions | 60 | 3.3 | 11 | 17.2 | 139 | 66.2 | 108 | 61.4 |
| Totals | 1,812 | 100.0 | 64 | 100.0 | 210 | 100.0 | 176 | 100.0 |

10.8 percent in the 0-to-19th percentile. The proportion of freshmen falling within the 80-to-99th percentile was two-and-one-half times as large for regular-admission as for special-admission freshmen.

*SAT Scores.* On the one hand, the mean SAT mathematics score for the regularly admitted freshmen was 502. The range was 250 through 749. The mean verbal score was 457, with the same range. The special-admission freshmen, on the other hand, had a mean SAT mathematics score of 346. The SAT verbal score mean was 315. The range for both scores was 200 through 549.

The regularly admitted freshmen compared favorably with the entire New Jersey college-bound population. The mean SAT math score for this larger population was 467, and the mean SAT verbal score was 425.

## Outcomes Assessment in New Jersey

In response to the national movement to assess higher education, the State of New Jersey developed the College Outcomes Evaluation Program (COEP). The Board of Higher Education appointed an advisory committee in 1985 for COEP, consisting of students, faculty, administrators, members of the business community, government, and the nonprofit sector. Its charge was to recommend to the chancellor of the state higher education system how best to design and institute a comprehensive system of evaluating the outcomes of the New Jersey colleges.

The advisory committee divided into subcommittees to investigate assessment of college outcomes within the state. The subcommittees included Student Learning; Student Development; Research, Scholarship, and Creative Expression; and Community-Society Impact subcommittees.

In 1987, after two years of deliberation the advisory committee made several recommendations, which were accepted by the chancellor and the Board of Higher Education (Montclair State College, 1987, pp. iv-v). The committee made eight recommendations:

1. A common statewide assessment of general intellectual skills at each institution
2. Assessment by each institution of the specific outcomes of its general educational program
3. An assessment of student learning in each major course of study prior to graduation by the faculty in each program, department, or discipline
4. Assessment of student development
5. An assessment of both the personal development of each institution's students and the degree of their satisfaction and involvement with their institutions
6. An assessment of the outcomes of each institution's faculty efforts in the areas of research, scholarship, and creative expression
7. An assessment of each institution's success in providing access and meeting the human-resource needs of its populations, as well as its economic impact on the community
8. Finally, an assessment of each institution's impacts on the community it serves through its mission and goals.

## Outcomes Assessment at Montclair State College

In response to the directives of the governor and the chancellor, the president of Montclair State College established an advisory committee on college outcomes evaluation in December 1986. It was a small working committee composed of faculty, staff, and administrators. He charged the committee to review the literature on college-outcomes assessment and study outcomes-assessment programs currently in operation or being developed on other campuses. He asked the committee to consider the issues raised by outcomes assessment as they affect state colleges such as Montclair. Finally, he requested that the committee make recommendations no later than April 1, 1987, on policies and actions regarding outcomes assessment.

The committee's report to the president stressed that Montclair needed to preserve its autonomy and uniqueness and therefore had to establish an assessment program that was faculty-initiated, not state-mandated. However, the committee stressed that regardless of the threat of state intrusion, outcomes assessment was an invaluable tool for institutional renewal and improvement.

Finally, the report noted that as a small working group with limited time, the committee could not recommend an assessment plan. The committee therefore recommended that a broad-based committee of faculty, administrators, and staff be appointed immediately to recommend an outcomes assessment model for Montclair. The president appointed a new, larger task force, and its subsequent report enumerated principles of assessment for Montclair State College, including that

• The primary goal of outcomes assessment be to improve programs and services
• Outcomes assessment not be used to evaluate individual faculty
• Faculty and nonteaching professionals assume primary responsibility for the development, implementation, and management of outcomes assessment
• Outcomes assessment employ multiple means of evaluation.

## Minority Students and Assessment

As Montclair begins to put its assessment plan into practice, it begins to question the effect of assessment on minority students. Despite the ever-increasing volume of literature on outcomes assessment, little of it deals with its impact on minorities.

The main argument against research on assessment and minorities is that the focus of assessment is the improvement of academic programs, not the measurement of student achievement. However, improvement of programs means better student achievement, and minority students may achieve different things in different ways. Are minority students attaining the goals and objectives that our assessment programs are measuring? Are these students reaching the competencies that institutions define as measures of success? Which assessment instruments are appropriate for minorities? Under which assessment alternatives are minorities successful?

The research community needs not only to ask these questions but to obtain the answers, not only for moral reasons but for the institutional survival of our colleges. As the proportion of minorities rises within an institution, institutional success depends increasingly on minority success. In many urban cities, the majority of public school children are minorities. Because of low average ages of minorities and high birth rates, the numbers of minorities will continue to increase. More children will be from multicultural backgrounds and will be more linguistically diverse, poorer, and educated in the less affluent school systems. By the year 2000, one out of every three people in the U.S. will be minority (Hodgkinson, 1985). As these children are born and mature they will proceed through the educational system. Much of the nation's success, not to mention the survival of many institutions of higher learning, will depend on preparing them for and attracting them to postsecondary education.

In New Jersey, the state-system chancellor has urged the state colleges to strive toward the goal of minority enrollment and performance on a par with those of White students. His reports have predicted that between 1990 and 2000 the non-White population of New Jersey will increase by 87 percent and that non-Whites are expected to constitute 26 percent of all 15 to 24 year olds (New Jersey Department of Higher Education, 1988).

Montclair State College services areas that are highly affected by the changing population. In 1987, approximately one-third of the high school graduates of its core counties were minorities: 19.9 percent were Blacks, 11.6 percent were Latinos, and 3.6 percent were Asians or Pacific Islanders.

The changing demographics of the counties Montclair serves becomes more evident in the population projections for the fifteen-to-twenty-four-year-old age cohort up to the year 2000. In all core counties, this cohort is projected to increase for minorities while that for the majority population is expected to decrease (New Jersey, Department of Labor, 1985). In short, the changing population of the counties Montclair serves will have a major impact on the institution. The college must change if it is to continue to serve its surrounding community.

In implementing outcomes assessment, given these demographic conditions, the committee members who are preparing or selecting assessment instruments, and especially the researcher, need to be sensitive to the following items:

• The assessment reports will need to define operationally the level of performance our students are expected to achieve within our programs. The rationale for each level and operational definition must be clear and valid.

• The minority sample gathered for institutional research should be broken down into the specific minority cohorts prevalent in the institution. Researchers do not obtain full, accurate information if they lump minorities together under generic terms like "Latinos," "Asians," or "minorities." For example, Lee (1985) found that Cubans approached Whites in terms of achievement, college enrollment, and educational ambition. Cubans had a higher family income, higher parental education, and a lower percentage of single-parent households than the Black population or any other Latino subgroup.

Montclair and similar state colleges will need to know which subgroups it serves, to assess the individual needs of the various subgroups, and to examine each constituency to determine how its members are performing in the educational process of the institution.

• In order to obtain sufficient data, researchers must oversample minority students. In most cases, all minority students will need to be included in the assessment research.

• Once the assessment has been conducted, researchers must explore whether any low levels of minority performance arose because the measurements contain cultural biases, whether the measurement instrument is valid, and whether the types of instruments being used are adequate to the assessment task. Since research indicates that minority students generally score lower than White students on standardized tests, Montclair will need to ensure that multiple measures of assessment are used, in order to obtain accurate information. In addition we should explore the possibility of nontraditional methods of assessment.

• If criterion-referenced instruments are used, one needs to ensure that the tests have been geared to the curriculum. Has the curriculum been accurately assessed? Has the information been delivered in the same ways to all students? Are we testing students on what we have taught? Have we explored the different learning styles of minority students? We will need to make sure that we are not placing students at a disadvantage.

• Finally, once the analyses have been conducted, one needs to review the programs that are not successful. If students are not meeting the level defined, how can the program be improved to change the outcome? Why are students not reaching the expected level? Is it because we are not doing what is necessary in our programs to help students succeed? The answer is not to lower our standards but to ensure that the program and institution are doing everything possible so that students can learn effectively and demonstrate that they have done so.

### References

Ewell, P. T. "Establishing a Campus-Based Assessment Program." In D. F. Halpern (ed.), *Student Outcomes Assessment: What Institutions Stand to Gain.* New Directions for Higher Education, no. 59. San Francisco: Jossey-Bass, 1987.

Hodgkinson, H. *All One System.* Washington, D.C.: Institute for Educational Leadership, 1985.

Latino Commission of Tri State. *Outlook.* New York: United Way of Tri State and Regional Plan Association, 1988.

Lee, V. *Access to Higher Education. The Experience of Blacks, Hispanics and Low Socio-Economic Status Whites.* Washington, D.C.: American Council on Education, 1985.

Montclair State College. *Report to the New Jersey Board of Higher Education from the Advisory Committee to the College Outcomes Evaluation Program.* Upper Montclair, N.J.: Montclair State College, 1987.

Montclair State College. *Report of the President Task Force on Outcomes Assessment.* Upper Montclair, N.J.: Montclair State College, 1988.

Montclair State College, Office of Institutional Research. *Statistical Profile of Montclair State College.* Upper Montclair, N.J.: Montclair State College, 1988.

New Jersey Department of Higher Education. *Vital Educational Statistics. Volume 1: 1984–85.* Trenton: New Jersey Department of Higher Education, 1985.

New Jersey Department of Higher Education. *Vital Educational Statistics. Volume 1: 1985–86.* Trenton: New Jersey Department of Higher Education, 1986.

New Jersey Department of Higher Education. *Improving Undergraduate Education.* Trenton: New Jersey Department of Higher Education, 1988a.

New Jersey Department of Higher Education. *Increasing Minority Education.* Trenton: New Jersey Department of Higher Education, 1988b.

New Jersey Department of Higher Education. *Vital Educational Statistics. Volume 1: 1987–88.* Trenton: New Jersey Department of Higher Education, 1988c.

New Jersey Department of Labor. *Population Projections for New Jersey and Counties 1990–2020.* Trenton, N.J.: Division of Planning and Research, Office of Demographic and Economic Analysis, 1985.

*Mildred Garcia is assistant vice-president for academic affairs and adjunct faculty in the Management Department, Montclair State College, New Jersey.*

*Florida has raised both minority expectations and minority achievement.*

# The Effects of Assessment on Minority Participation and Achievement in Higher Education

*Roy E. McTarnaghan*

External assessment of Florida colleges and universities has been developing throughout the 1980s. At the beginning of the decade, state legislation mandated secondary-school completion examinations, collectively referred to as the "Functional Literacy Exam." By 1980, following gradual expansion of the secondary-school curriculum, analyses had revealed that a smaller proportion of college-bound students—both minority and nonminority—were enrolling in traditional college preparatory courses than ten years earlier. This led the Florida Board of Regents to significantly increase admissions standards for freshmen entering the state university system in 1981, phasing the standards in over a five-year period.

The higher academic-unit standards were accompanied by increased score requirements on the American College Test (ACT) and Scholastic Aptitude Test (SAT) admissions exams. Through the 1978 plan submitted by Florida and accepted by the United States Office for Civil Rights to increase minority participation in postsecondary education, secondary schools and colleges introduced special counseling and support programs to assist in securing higher minority participation.

## College Level Academic Skills Test

In the early 1980s, legislation was enacted in Florida for a rising junior examination in communication and computation, to be developed jointly by community-college and university faculty. By 1984 the assessment exam

New Directions for Institutional Research, no. 65, Spring 1990 © Jossey-Bass Inc., Publishers

was in place with acceptable passing scores required for students to move into the junior year in college. While exceptions have allowed students to continue in college after passing only three of the four test subsections, students must pass all sections of the test in order to graduate.

Passing score rates for the College Level Academic Skills Test (CLAST) examination have been raised in 1986 and again in 1989. The passing rates by race under the 1982 standards are shown in Table 1.

In the fall of 1986, a new, higher passing score was implemented. In that year, the passing rates for all four subtests were 65 percent for Blacks, 84 percent for Latinos, and 92 percent for Whites. Essentially, the increases occurred even against higher standards due to precollege preparation (see Table 2) and careful attention to course placement in college as part of the orientation process.

## Strengthening Secondary-School Requirements

In 1981, convinced that too many entering freshmen were not prepared to succeed in higher education, the Florida Board of Regents used the admissions standard as a way of providing leverage for high schools to help students. Too many students had been enrolled in postsecondary remedial or developmental programs, and many did not last in college.

A major problem was that students had not taken enough college-preparatory courses. The Board of Regents implemented stronger requirements, including additional math beyond the level of algebra 1, additional science with laboratory experience, and English with substantial writing, and recommended a foreign-language requirement. Several universities in the nine-campus system objected, and many public-school leaders complained that the requirements would cause severe staffing disruptions. However, the initial two years of this plan were so successful that in 1983 the Florida legislature enacted into law similar provisions for a broader range of students than just those applying to the state university system.

In the 1987–88 academic year, of the 14,606 students enrolled as first-time-in-college students in the State University System of Florida, 528 students (3.6 percent) in reading, 359 (2.5 percent) in writing, and 789

**Table 1. Minority Passing Rate for the CLAST under 1982 Standards**

|  | Passing Rate (in %) | | |
| Year | Black | Latino | White |
| --- | --- | --- | --- |
| 1982 | 35 | 53 | 80 |
| 1986 | 73 | 90 | 93 |

(5.4 percent) in mathematics fell below cutoff scores and were placed in noncredit developmental courses.

Table 2 compares the increase in traditional college-preparatory courses before and after the admissions rule went into effect. These data show that the entering students were certainly much better prepared to be successful in college.

Table 3, which compares the change in high school grade-point averages, indicates that the higher levels of expectation also produced a better grade-point average. Some would have thought otherwise due to the larger number of students now in the applicant and admitted pools who, just a few years earlier, would not have enrolled. During the 1980s, the Florida twelfth-grade enrollment has been essentially flat, while the number of new students entering Florida's state university system has been growing—for both Whites and Blacks.

Tables 4 and 5 show changes in SAT and ACT scores, respectively, for entering students in Florida's state university system. Compared with almost any state system, these positive changes are dramatic. They could not have occurred without a statewide mandate for all college-bound students to become better prepared prior to high school graduation. That these students also demonstrated success once admitted can be seen in Table 6, where the increase in retention between the beginning of the first and second years of college was 24 percent, from 60 percent to 84 percent of all first time college students taking a full load of at least 12 credits per term.

While the challenge has been to increase the academic preparation of students, there has been a parallel move to counsel high school students to understand the advantages of higher education and the opportunities available to college graduates. From a Florida high school survey

**Table 2. Public High School Students Taking College Prep Courses**

| Courses | Fall '80 (%) | Fall '86 (%) |
|---|---|---|
| 4 years English | 75 | 80 |
| 3 years social studies | 72 | 93 |
| 3 years mathematics | 91 | 99 |
| 2 years foreign language | 58 | 87 |

**Table 3. State University System of Florida Entering Freshman Grade-Point Averages from College-Prep High School Courses**

| 1980 | 1981 | 1982 | 1983 | 1984 | 1985 | 1986 | 1987 |
|---|---|---|---|---|---|---|---|
| 2.97 | 2.98 | 3.03 | 3.00 | 3.01 | 3.08 | 3.12 | 3.13 |

**Table 4. State University System of Florida Average SAT Scores of Entering Freshmen**

| 1980 | 1981 | 1982 | 1983 | 1984 | 1985 | 1986 | 1987 |
|------|------|------|------|------|------|------|------|
| 957  | 976  | 1010 | 1012 | 1007 | 1025 | 1028 | 1043 |

**Table 5. State University System of Florida Average ACT Scores of Entering Freshmen**

| 1980 | 1981 | 1982 | 1983 | 1984 | 1985 | 1986 | 1987 |
|------|------|------|------|------|------|------|------|
| 20.9 | 21.7 | 22.4 | 22.3 | 22.2 | 22.5 | 22.5 | 22.8 |

**Table 6. State University System of Florida Retention of Freshmen Through the First Year**

| Status   | 1980–81 | 1984–85 |
|----------|---------|---------|
| Retention | 60%     | 84%     |
| Drop-Out  | 40%     | 16%     |

conducted every two years since 1983, Table 7 shows a positive change in attitude among minority youth, who have been under-represented in postsecondary enrollment.

Among the nine Florida universities, Florida A&M University (FAMU), with a majority Black-student enrollment, enrolled 481 freshmen in 1981 with an average score of 749 on the SAT. By 1987, FAMU had more freshmen (652) and SAT average scores increased to 798—a 49-point score gain.

High school grades, number of college-preparatory courses taken, entrance-exam scores, and retention in college rose during the 1980s among both secondary students and college students in Florida. This could not have occurred so dramatically without a single governing board purposely strengthening academic standards through the admissions process. The 1981 cry that "it can't be done" has now been silenced.

Experience has shown that minority youth, as well as Whites, need to be in a college-preparatory program to be successful in higher education. Further, selecting the right admissions criteria is essential. Florida's evidence shows that success on admissions tests in math depends on having completed algebra—a necessary prerequisite for many curriculum areas. As more minority youth are counseled into the college-preparatory track, not the vocational track, their success rate in college goes up, and the open door to college does not become for them a "revolving door": quickly in and quickly out.

**Table 7.  Percentage of Florida White, Black, and Latino High School Students Expressing the Desire to Enroll in a Four-Year College**

|         | 1983 | 1985 | 1987 |
|---------|------|------|------|
| White   | 37.2 | 32.5 | 35.1 |
| Black   | 28.8 | 34.1 | 39.2 |
| Latino  | 26.2 | 36.4 | 37.4 |

The evidence in Florida clearly shows that a state can reverse years of academic neglect with foresight and strong leadership at the governing-board level.

## Participation and Achievement

During the two-year period from 1985 to 1987, the number of high school graduates in Florida increased by 3 percent. During that same period, Black high school graduates decreased by 3 percent, Latino graduates increased by 5 percent, and other minorities increased by 26 percent.

During this two-year period, Black first-time college students in Florida's state university system increased by 38 percent, from 2,531 to 3,483. Latinos increased by 40 percent, from 1,310 to 1,843, and other minorities increased by 41 percent, from 535 to 752.

These data suggest that efforts in public schools and higher education to encourage more minorities to enter the college-preparatory curriculum have paid dividends. A number of specially funded programs in Florida have been directed toward early intervention and counseling for minorities, both in the schools and through community agencies. These programs continue as a long-term commitment of the state to increase minority college-participation rates to equal their share of the high school graduating population.

Examining retention of students in school by way of baccalaureate-degree completions between 1984–85 and 1986–87, inclusive, we see that total degrees awarded increased by 0.6 percent, from 20,312 to 20,431. Among Blacks, degrees earned declined 4 percent, from 1,396 to 1,344. Among Latinos, there was an 11-percent increase from 1,371 to 1,528. Other minorities showed a 10-percent increase, from 319 to 350.

In Table 8, an analysis of the first-time CLAST examinees from the fall of 1986, who were followed through five subsequent test administrations, shows that minority-passing performance was still below majority-passing performance.

While minority admissions and one-year retention rates are up, there clearly are problems with retention from the second year through graduation. The rate of success among Blacks and other minorities on the

CLAST test suggests that more attention must be paid to placement testing and counseling throughout the experience of higher education of these students in order to increase their graduation rate to equal the gains shown on the entering characteristics of them as freshmen.

## Conclusion

Projecting the direction of student performance and achievement and the effect of policy on performance are often difficult because of uncertainties about human motivation and behavior. Who, for example, would predict that raising admissions and retention standards would lead to better academic access, performance, and achievement by minority students? Present data show that minority students are under-represented among the new entrants to college and over-represented among the underprepared and drop-outs. However, the more demanding assessment policies in the state of Florida have yielded favorable results because they have focused on the skill levels needed for academic success and on the need for college-preparatory counseling in the middle schools and junior high schools.

Table 8. Cumulative Percentage of Students Passing After Indicated-Administration College Level Academic Skills Test—1986 Cohort

|  | September 1986 | June 1988 |
|---|---|---|
| All | 82.2 | 93.4 |
| White | 88.9 | 96.1 |
| Black | 50.7 | 81.7 |
| Latino | 75.1 | 92.1 |
| Other | 57.8 | 81.9 |

*Roy E. McTarnaghan is executive vice-chancellor and academic vice-chancellor of the State University System of Florida.*

*Minority students are substantially disadvantaged in mathematics, and students of all races score low enough to jeopardize future U.S. leadership in science and technology.*

# How Prepared Are Our Minority Students for College-Level Mathematics?

*Janet R. Johnson*

A variety of national, state, and local councils, boards, and commissions have spent considerable effort over the past few years examining the educational development of American youngsters. The central focus has been upon the effectiveness of American elementary and secondary schools compared with schools in other nations and on the effectiveness of America's schools in preparing students for postsecondary education and work. Study groups have used the intellectual readiness and competitive acumen of the nation's youth as indicators of school effectiveness as well as to project future economic, social, and scientific developments in the United States. The results of the National Assessment of Educational Progress (NAEP) add factual data and information to the ongoing debates about the intellectual preparedness of American youth for higher education and for employment.

The National Assessment of Educational Progress has been conducting assessments of America's school-age children since 1969 and has surveyed approximately 1.3 million students in a variety of subject areas such as reading, writing, mathematics, and science. Currently, NAEP assesses about 100,000 students in three grades and ages (grade 4, age 9; grade 8, age 13; and grade 12, age 17) every two years. Each administration covers several subject areas and includes both open-ended and multiple-choice questions covering a wide range of content and process areas within each subject. Information is also gathered during each administration that permits analyses of school, home, and attitudinal factors in addition to students' knowledge and abilities. Data and information about the backgrounds, behaviors, and attitudes of students and characteristics of their community and school help to identify important factors related to their performance. Institutional researchers can use NAEP data to prepare colleges and universities for the next generation of college students.

This chapter focuses on mathematics as an essential component of informed citizenship. *Integrity in the College Curriculum: A Report to the Academic Community* (1985) makes one of the more powerful and compelling arguments for the importance of mathematics in the college curriculum and in today's society:

> We have become a society bombarded by numbers. We are threatened by them. We are intimidated by them. We are lied to with their help. We are comforted by them and seduced by them. . . . Numbers are not neutral. They are not inert. They are as alive as we are when they greet us and we greet them: they become what we understand them to be. For that reason, in a world of numbers students should encounter concepts that permit a sophisticated response to arguments and positions which depend on numbers and statistics. Such concepts would include degree of risk, scatter, uncertainty, orders of magnitude, rates of change, confidence levels and acceptability, and the interpretation of graphs as they are manifest in numbers. Citizens intellectually comfortable with these concepts would, among other things, be less vulnerable to the misuse of numbers by advertisers and political candidates [p. 17].

This chapter presents 1985–86 mathematics proficiency, background, and attitudinal data for age seventeen, grade eleven students with an emphasis on Black and Hispanic students, and discusses such trends over four assessment cycles. While the results of the NAEP are interesting and important, the primary reason they are presented here is to provide an example of how NAEP results can be useful in institutional research and planning for ethnic diversity. NAEP results can help inform college and university decisions on a variety of issues including, for example, specific remediation program needs and retention programs. The results for the eleventh-graders are based on a national probability sample of approximately 12,000 students. To illustrate trends, a sample of approximately 4,000 additional seventeen-year-old students were selected in the 1985–86 assessment. This sample permits comparisons with past assessment data which, prior to 1983, was collected on age seventeen students rather than grade eleven students. Comparing the results of age seventeen assessments over time permits detection of changes in the educational attainments of the nation's seventeen-year-olds. Table 1 provides a detailed breakdown by ethnicity or race and also provides estimates of general student population characteristics. (Please note that this chapter refers to "Hispanics" rather than "Latinos" because the data collection instrument used the former term.)

**Table 1. Breakdown by Race or Ethnicity of Numbers of
Grade Eleven and Age Seventeen Students in Mathematics Sample
and General Population**

|  | No. of Students in the Sample for Mathematics | No. of Students in the Population (estimated) |
|---|---|---|
| Grade Eleven | | |
| Total | 11,850 | 3.2 million |
| White | 8,389 | 2.4 million |
| Black | 1,918 | 420 thousand |
| Hispanic | 1,185 | 240 thousand |
| Other | 358 | 110 thousand |
| Age Seventeen | | |
| Total | 3,868 | 3.2 million |
| White | 2,749 | 2.5 million |
| Black | 671 | 460 thousand |
| Hispanic | 332 | 180 thousand |
| Other | 116 | 84 thousand |

*Source:* Burke and others, 1987.

## The NAEP Scale

The NAEP data have been analyzed using Item Response Theory (IRT) scaling technology and are summarized on a common scale (0 to 500) to facilitate direct comparisons between assessment years for age groups and subpopulations. To provide a basis for interpreting the results, NAEP describes what students attaining different proficiency levels on the scale are able to do.

The assessment defines five levels of proficiency:

1. Level 150—simple arithmetic facts
2. Level 200—beginning skills and understanding
3. Level 250—basic operations and beginning problem solving
4. Level 300—moderately complex procedures and reasoning
5. Level 350—multi-step problem solving and algebra.

The NAEP mathematics scale is a weighted composite of proficiency on five content area subscales; knowledge and skills, higher-level applications, measurement, geometry, and algebra (Dossey, Mullis, Lindquist, and Chambers, 1988).

## Definitions of NAEP Proficiency Levels

*Level 150—Simple Arithmetic Facts.* Learners at this level know some basic facts about addition and subtraction, and most can add two-digit numbers without regrouping. They recognize simple situations in which addition and subtraction apply. They also are developing rudimentary classification skills.

*Level 200—Beginning Skills and Understanding.* Learners at this level have considerable understanding of two-digit numbers. They can add two-digit numbers but are still developing an ability to regroup in subtraction. They know some basic facts about multiplication and division, recognize relations between coins, can read information from charts and graphs, and can use simple measurement instruments. They are developing some reasoning skills.

*Level 250—Basic Operations and Beginning Problem Solving.* Learners at this level have an initial understanding of the four basic arithmetic operations. They are able to apply whole-number addition and subtraction skills to one-step word problems and money situations. In multiplication they can find the product of a two-digit and a one-digit number. They can also compare information from graphs and charts and are developing an ability to analyze simple logical relations.

*Level 300—Moderately Complex Procedures and Reasoning.* Learners at this level are developing an understanding of number systems. They can compute with decimals, simple fractions, and commonly encountered percents. They can identify geometrical figures, measure lengths and angles, and calculate areas of rectangles. These students are also able to interpret simple inequalities, evaluate formulas, and solve simple linear equations. They can find averages, make decisions on information drawn from graphs, and use logical reasoning to solve problems. They are developing the skills to operate with signed numbers, exponents, and square roots.

*Level 350—Multi-Step Problem Solving and Algebra.* Learners at this level can apply a range of reasoning skills to solve multi-step problems. They can solve routine problems involving fractions and percents, recognize properties of basic geometrical figures, and work with exponents and square roots. They can solve a variety of two-step problems using variables, identify equivalent algebraic expressions, and solve linear equations and inequalities. They are developing an understanding of functions and coordinate systems.

Dossey and colleagues (1988) provide a number of example items that were actually administered in the 1985–86 assessment and that are reflective of each of the levels described above.

## Minority-Student Proficiency at Each Level

Essentially all of eleventh-grade Black and Hispanic students reach Levels 150 and 200. These students are able to perform basic arithmetic but have difficulty with reasoning that requires more than simple numerical computation. Eighty-six percent of Black, 92 percent of Hispanic, and 99 percent of White eleventh-graders can respond successfully to items at or above Level 250, which requires whole-number computation skills and reflects a level of knowledge and understanding generally associated with middle or junior high school mathematics.

At Level 300, minority performance drops dramatically, with 22 percent of Black, 28 percent of Hispanic, and 63 percent of White eleventh-graders performing at or above Level 300. This level involves decimals, simple fractions, and percents as well as some geometry and algebra. Exposure to many of the topics at this level usually occurs in middle or junior high school.

Level 350 involves a somewhat more sophisticated level of mathematical understanding and manipulation. For example, it includes multistep problem solving, linear equations and inequalities, and exponents and square roots. In other words, Level 350 includes the basic building blocks for higher level mathematics. Unfortunately, very few Black, Hispanic, or White students achieve Level 350. Only one-half of 1 percent of Black, 1 percent of Hispanic, and 7 percent of White eleventh-graders successfully respond to questions in mathematics at this level. (An interesting side note concerning Asian students, but one that requires extreme caution in interpretation due to small sample size, is that approximately 23 percent of the Asian population of eleventh-graders achieve Level 350.) To the extent that higher-level mathematics is an important tool for daily life and work, the implications for the majority of the population and their future well-being in college or the work-force are staggering. Because Level 350 includes the skills and understanding associated with the basic building blocks for higher-level mathematics, NAEP data imply that a large percentage of college freshmen will require remedial programs to bring their skills up to an appropriate level for college work in mathematics.

## Trends over Time in Minority-Student Proficiency at Each Level

NAEP trend data in mathematics are available on an age-only sample of in-school seventeen-year-olds from four assessments administered in 1972–73, 1977–78, 1981–82, and 1985–86. Table 2 below provides comparative percentage for age seventeen White, Black, and Hispanic students by performance levels in three of the four assessment years (the 1973 data were not included in the NAEP trend data scaling). Because virtually all students in each racial or ethnic group performed at or above Level 150 in all NAEP math assessments, Table 2 begins with Level 200.

Table 2 shows considerable improvement over the past decade in seventeen-year-old minority student performance at Level 250. State and school initiatives toward improving basic mathematical skills have appar-

**Table 2. Percentages of Students at or Above the Proficiency Levels
by Year and Ethnicity/Race**

|  | Percentages | | |
|---|---|---|---|
| Ethnicity or Race | 1977–78 | 1981–82 | 1985–86 |
| Level 200 | | | |
| White | 100.0 (0.0) | 100.0 (0.0) | 99.9 (0.0) |
| Black | 98.7 (0.2) | 99.6 (0.2) | 100.0 (0.0) |
| Hispanic | 99.3 (0.2) | 99.9 (0.1) | 98.9 (1.1) |
| Level 250 | | | |
| White | 95.8 (0.3) | 96.3 (0.3) | 98.3 (0.2) |
| Black | 70.0 (1.4) | 75.3 (1.3) | 86.0 (1.7) |
| Hispanic | 77.4 (2.2) | 81.3 (1.0) | 90.8 (2.1) |
| Level 300 | | | |
| White | 57.3 (1.1) | 54.5 (1.3) | 58.0 (1.4) |
| Black | 18.0 (1.3) | 17.3 (1.5) | 21.7 (2.6) |
| Hispanic | 22.1 (2.4) | 20.6 (2.2) | 26.8 (3.9) |
| Level 350 | | | |
| White | 8.6 (0.4) | 6.3 (0.5) | 7.6 (0.5) |
| Black | 0.4 (0.2) | 0.6 (0.2) | 0.3 (0.2) |
| Hispanic | 1.1 (0.4) | 0.5 (0.2) | 1.2 (0.6) |

*Note:* Standard errors are in parentheses.

ently been working. Average mathematics proficiency has improved over
the decade but only at the low end. The proportion of students achieving
Level 300 or above has remained relatively flat. These data indicate that
more than 70 percent of this nation's future Black and Hispanic citizens
and workers hold only a minimal understanding of the basic mathematical operations of addition, subtraction, multiplication, and division.

If the impetus to improve such basic skills diminishes, college and
university faculties will find no mathematical foundation on which to
build. How will students, or the nation, forge ahead in a competitive
world and work-place? What will be their quality of life? We must engage
the interest and imagination of all our students and foster continued
achievement in the more complex mathematical fields.

## Trends over Time in Patterns of Course Taking
## by Minorities

Data for seventeen-year-olds for each of the previous three assessments
allow us to track over time the highest level of math coursework taken by
each ethnic or racial group. Table 3, below, summarizes these data.

Table 3 shows that students are taking more math courses. For example, fewer seventeen-year-olds in all groups in 1985–86 reported stopping their mathematical education with pre-algebra than in prior years. There has been a noticeable increase over the years in the number of Hispanic students who complete algebra, geometry, algebra 2, and calculus. However, significantly fewer Black and Hispanic seventeen-year-olds complete algebra 2 than is true of White students. However, for no ethnic or racial group could the math course attainment level be described as stellar. Fifty-four percent of the eleventh-grade population in this country have stopped their math training even before reaching the algebra-2 level, and another forty percent stop with algebra 2. The low percentage of any group of students reaching the calculus level severely undermines the prospects for scientific and technological research in the United States.

These data also hold implications for colleges. Forty percent of Hispanic and 53 percent of both Black and White eleventh-graders across the

**Table 3. Percentages of Seventeen-Year-Olds Reporting Highest Level of Mathematics Course Taken**

| | Percentages | | |
|---|---|---|---|
| Ethnicity or Race | 1977–78 | 1981–82 | 1985–86 |
| Pre-Algebra | | | |
| White | 19.6 (1.1) | 22.0 (1.4) | 16.8 (1.0) |
| Black | 33.5 (1.4) | 34.3 (2.2) | 30.7 (2.8) |
| Hispanic | 38.4 (3.2) | 37.3 (4.0) | 24.6 (2.4) |
| Algebra | | | |
| White | 16.6 (0.6) | 15.2 (0.6) | 17.2 (0.9) |
| Black | 19.4 (1.2) | 19.8 (1.9) | 17.8 (1.7) |
| Hispanic | 18.6 (2.1) | 21.3 (2.4) | 24.0 (2.7) |
| Geometry | | | |
| White | 17.4 (0.7) | 14.8 (0.8) | 16.7 (1.1) |
| Black | 11.2 (0.8) | 10.4 (1.0) | 15.6 (2.2) |
| Hispanic | 12.3 (1.2) | 11.6 (1.3) | 15.8 (3.0) |
| Algebra 2 | | | |
| White | 39.1 (1.3) | 41.1 (1.5) | 42.2 (1.4) |
| Black | 28.3 (2.0) | 29.0 (2.3) | 30.9 (1.6) |
| Hispanic | 22.6 (2.7) | 24.4 (2.4) | 27.9 (2.7) |
| Calculus | | | |
| White | 5.6 (0.4) | 5.4 (0.5) | 6.7 (0.8) |
| Black | 4.4 (0.5) | 3.8 (0.8) | 2.9 (0.8) |
| Hispanic | 3.4 (0.9) | 3.3 (0.6) | 6.1 (1.8) |

*Note:* Standard errors are in parentheses.

country who took the mathematics assessment plan to enter a four-year college after high school. Another 24 percent of Hispanic, 19 percent of Black, and 21 percent of White eleventh-graders report that they are interested in entering a two-year college after graduating from high school. Given that the NAEP data on science, reading, and writing are as dismal as the data on mathematics, it suggests that current remedial programs at the college level will become an even more important and necessary part of the curriculum than they are at present.

## A Profile of Life Outside of School

In addition to the achievement levels and college aspirations of the high school population, the NAEP data can help us understand better what the upcoming pool of potential college students will be like.

One of the standard demographic reporting categories that National Assessment uses is size and type of community (STOC), which classifies schools by the residential distribution and parental occupation of attending students. The seven STOC categories are as follows: extreme rural, low metropolitan (extreme inner city), high metropolitan (extreme affluent suburb), main big city (remainder of big city), urban fringe (suburban fringe), medium city, and small places (small city) (Burke and others, 1987). Fifty-seven percent of Black, 59 percent of Hispanic, and 38 percent of White eleventh-graders live in or on the fringe of a big city. High metropolitan, or advantaged urban, accounts for 14 percent of the total eleventh-grade student population, including 18 percent of Blacks, 10 percent of Hispanics, and 15 percent of Whites. Low metropolitan, or disadvantaged urban, accounts for 5 percent of the total eleventh-grade student population, with 18 percent of Blacks and Hispanics and 2 percent of Whites. As illustrated in Table 4, high metropolitan students score at least 25 points higher than low metropolitan students regardless of ethnicity or race. White eleventh-graders score at least nineteen points higher than their minority counterparts in *both* low and high metropolitan areas. Nearly a quarter of all Black eleventh-graders (23 percent) live in medium-sized cities as compared with 10 percent of Hispanic eleventh-graders, while slightly more than a quarter of the Hispanic students (27 percent) live in small cities.

Another standard reporting category is region of the country. Table 5 illustrates eleventh-grade student population concentration and proficiency scores by region across the country. The largest concentration of Black eleventh-graders is in the southeast and exhibits the lowest math scores of all groups. The largest concentration of Hispanic eleventh-graders is in the west.

NAEP also collects information from students about their parents' education. Black parents were reported to have less education than White parents, and Hispanic parents had substantially less than Black. Table 6 shows that 11 percent of White eleventh-graders report having mothers who did not graduate from high school, rising to 16 percent of Black and 32 percent of Hispanic eleventh-graders. As for college graduation rates, 22 percent of Black and 25 percent of White, as compared with 13 percent of Hispanic eleventh-graders, report that their mother graduated from college. Between those whose mothers graduated from high school and those whose mothers graduated from college, there is a 14-point difference in the proficiency scores for both Black and Hispanic students and a 16-point difference for White students.

Table 7 presents data for fathers' education. Twenty-seven percent of Hispanic, 15 percent of Black, and 13 percent of White eleventh-graders reported having fathers who had not graduated from high school. Eighteen percent of Hispanic, 21 percent of Black, and 35 percent of White students responding reported that their father had graduated from college. Between those whose fathers graduated from high school and those whose fathers graduated from college there is a 17-point difference in the proficiency scores for Black and White students and a 20-point difference for Hispanic students.

Table 8 presents data collected by NAEP on a variety of additional outside-of-school variables. Substantially fewer Black than White or Hispanic eleventh-graders live with both parents. Of all Black students more than one-third reside with their mother. Those students who live with both parents score 5 points (Hispanic students) to 7 points (Black students) higher than those who live with their mother only.

**Table 4. Size and Type of Community Membership and Proficiency**

| Ethnicity or Race | Rural | Low Met | High Met | Big City |
|---|---|---|---|---|
| White | 4.7 (1.7) | 1.6 (0.7) | 14.5 (2.7) | 5.1 (1.5) |
| | 305.0 (2.9) | 297.2 (4.8) | 321.7 (1.6) | 303.9 (1.7) |
| Black | 4.0 (2.3) | 18.2 (3.4) | 7.5 (1.5) | 18.1 (4.2) |
| | 269.7 (2.1) | 270.4 (3.0) | 302.7 (4.9) | 280.1 (2.3) |
| Hispanic | 3.6 (2.1) | 17.5 (4.5) | 10.4 (2.6) | 18.3 (4.1) |
| | 277.7 (6.4) | 278.5 (3.8) | 305.1 (3.8) | 285.7 (3.4) |

| Ethnicity or Race | Fringe | Med City | Small City |
|---|---|---|---|
| White | 16.4 (2.1) | 15.4 (2.6) | 42.4 (4.0) |
| | 307.4 (1.1) | 312.3 (1.5) | 306.8 (1.0) |
| Black | 12.5 (5.4) | 23.2 (3.7) | 16.5 (2.0) |
| | 283.9 (2.3) | 278.5 (2.0) | 276.8 (1.8) |
| Hispanic | 13.4 (3.4) | 9.5 (2.1) | 27.2 (5.6) |
| | 284.3 (3.8) | 282.8 (2.6) | 284.2 (2.9) |

*Note:* Standard errors are in parentheses.

### Table 5. Student Concentration and Proficiency Scores by Region

| Ethnicity or Race | N-East | S-East | Central | West |
|---|---|---|---|---|
| White | 25.6 (0.1) | 19.2 (1.8) | 32.3 (1.8) | 22.9 (0.1) |
| | 314.1 (1.5) | 305.6 (1.7) | 309.1 (1.2) | 307.9 (1.6) |
| Black | 23.8 (0.3) | 40.8 (0.3) | 19.5 (2.6) | 16.0 (2.6) |
| | 283.9 (2.6) | 274.7 (1.2) | 281.1 (4.1) | 280.7 (2.8) |
| Hispanic | 13.8 (2.0) | 6.7 (1.3) | 10.9 (2.3) | 68.5 (0.4) |
| | 290.0 (4.1) | 281.6 (3.9) | 282.6 (2.7) | 285.6 (2.0) |

*Note:* Standard errors are in parentheses.

### Table 6. Mothers' High School and College Graduation Rates and Student Proficiency Scores

| Ethnicity or Race | Some HS | Grad HS | Grad College | Don't Know |
|---|---|---|---|---|
| White | 11.2 (0.5) | 38.0 (0.9) | 24.7 (1.1) | 3.6 (0.2) |
| | 295.0 (1.3) | 305.0 (0.7) | 320.9 (0.9) | 288.3 (1.3) |
| Black | 16.3 (0.7) | 33.5 (0.8) | 21.9 (1.0) | 8.4 (0.6) |
| | 271.0 (1.4) | 275.6 (1.5) | 289.4 (2.2) | 271.4 (2.9) |
| Hispanic | 32.4 (2.3) | 27.0 (2.3) | 12.6 (0.7) | 14.3 (0.9) |
| | 280.0 (1.8) | 285.0 (1.7) | 298.7 (4.2) | 274.3 (2.5) |

*Note:* Standard errors are in parentheses.

### Table 7. Fathers' High School and College Graduation Rates and Student Proficiency Scores

| Ethnicity or Race | Some HS | Grad HS | Grad College | Don't Know |
|---|---|---|---|---|
| White | 13.2 (0.7) | 27.1 (0.9) | 34.9 (1.5) | 5.9 (0.3) |
| | 294.1 (1.4) | 303.7 (0.6) | 320.9 (0.8) | 292.2 (1.9) |
| Black | 15.0 (0.4) | 30.1 (0.8) | 20.7 (0.8) | 20.1 (0.8) |
| | 273.3 (1.5) | 275.3 (1.4) | 292.1 (2.5) | 270.4 (1.9) |
| Hispanic | 27.0 (1.7) | 23.2 (1.0) | 17.6 (1.3) | 19.1 (0.9) |
| | 280.5 (2.1) | 281.0 (1.8) | 301.2 (2.7) | 276.8 (2.0) |

*Note:* Standard errors are in parentheses.

It is worth noting that a large percentage of the Hispanic eleventh-grade students report that they speak a language other than English in the home and that a majority live in households where a language other than English is spoken at least half the time. However, no significant difference in mathematics-proficiency scores is attributable to living in a second-language situation.

Fewer than one half of all eleventh-graders come from households in which both parents work full-time. In 11 percent of the Hispanic households only the mother works (note, however, that 19 percent report living with mother only). In 18 percent of the Black households only the mother works (note, however, that 35 percent live with mother only). Black and Hispanic eleventh-graders score slightly higher in mathematics if both of their parents work full-time. This does not hold true for White eleventh-graders, who seem to do better if one parent works full-time and the other works part-time.

Very nearly a third of all minority eleventh-graders have four or more siblings and nearly a quarter have two siblings. Students with fewer siblings score ten points higher on the mathematics assessment.

Almost one-third of Hispanic students and more than one-fifth of Black students live in homes that have three or fewer of the following articles: newspaper, dictionary, magazines, encyclopedia, or twenty-five books; and fewer than one-half of Black and Hispanic eleventh-graders have all five items at home. The difference in the mathematics proficiency scores between those who have three or fewer and those who have all five is substantial (Black students—16 points; Hispanic students—18 points; and White students—20 points).

NAEP data appear to confirm the common wisdom that watching many hours of television adversely affects a student's academic proficiency. A majority of White students report watching up to two hours of television each day, while a majority of Black students watch between three and five hours per day. Math scores drop 25 points for White students, 20 points for Hispanics, and 16 points for Blacks between watching up to two hours and watching six or more hours of television daily.

Despite the pervasiveness of television viewing, a relatively large number of eleventh-graders work at a part-time job. Interestingly, there is no clear pattern associated with the number of hours worked and mathematics proficiency.

Regarding absence from school, the vast majority of eleventh-graders reported that they missed at the most three to four days of school last month. Those missing fewer than two days scored at least ten points higher on the math assessment than those missing more than two days.

## Eleventh-Grade Minority Student Attitudes Toward Mathematics

Table 9 presents NAEP data on the attitudes expressed by eleventh-graders toward mathematics.

## Table 8. Outside-of-School Environment

| | Percentages[1] | | |
|---|---|---|---|
| Variables | White | Black | Hispanic |
| Live with Both Parents | 82 | 56 | 72 |
| Live with Single Parent | 16 | 38 | 22 |
| Live with Mother Only | 13 | 35 | 19 |
| Live with Father Only | 3 | 3 | 3 |
| Both Parents Work Full-Time | 43 | 49 | 36 |
| One Full-Time, One Part-Time | 20 | 9 | 14 |
| Father Alone Works | 23 | 14 | 27 |
| Mother Alone Works | 9 | 18 | 11 |
| Have Four or More Siblings | 16 | 33 | 33 |
| Have Three Siblings | 16 | 17 | 20 |
| Have Two Siblings | 29 | 22 | 24 |
| Have One Sibling | 33 | 21 | 18 |
| Have No Siblings | 6 | 7 | 5 |
| Articles in the Home: Newspaper; Dictionary; Magazines; Encyclopedia; Twenty-Five Books | | | |
| Home Has Five | 67 | 49 | 39 |
| Home Has Four | 23 | 29 | 29 |
| Home Has Three or Fewer | 10 | 22 | 32 |
| Watch Six or More Hours TV Daily | 7 | 24 | 11 |
| Watch Three to Five Hours TV Daily | 42 | 54 | 48 |
| Watch Up to Two Hours TV Daily | 51 | 23 | 41 |
| Number of Hours Work Each Week in a Part-Time Job | | | |
| 22–25 | 8 | 5 | 6 |
| 16–20 | 13 | 8 | 11 |
| 11–15 | 10 | 5 | 6 |
| 6–10 | 9 | 9 | 9 |
| Fewer than 6 | 8 | 6 | 9 |
| None | 43 | 59 | 49 |
| Number of Days of School Missed Last Month | | | |
| More than 10 | 2 | 3 | 7 |
| 5–10 | 8 | 9 | 12 |
| 3–4 | 17 | 20 | 23 |
| 1–2 | 38 | 32 | 29 |
| 0–1 | 35 | 36 | 27 |

[1]Due to the categories "other" and "missing," percents will not equal 100.

## Table 9. Attitudes Toward Mathematics

| Variables | Percentages | | |
| --- | --- | --- | --- |
| | White | Black | Hispanic |
| Will work when older in an area that requires math | 45 | 51 | 48 |
| Need to use math to get along well in everyday life | 58 | 68 | 51 |
| It is important to know math such as algebra and geometry to get a good job | 49 | 72 | 62 |
| Are willing to work hard in math | 77 | 91 | 82 |
| Would like to take more math | 38 | 42 | 47 |
| Dislike math | 30 | 23 | 34 |
| Find math difficult | 46 | 37 | 43 |
| Undecided/do not like to be challenged when given a difficult math problem | 46 | 35 | 48 |
| Parents give great encouragement to take math courses | 46 | 58 | 55 |
| Get regular help with math homework from parents | 25 | 36 | 34 |
| Get regular help with math homework from friends | 50 | 58 | 55 |
| Spend less than one-hour a week on math homework | 50 | 49 | 52 |
| Understand what is being talked about in math class | 67 | 74 | 65 |
| Undecided/certain that math is made up of unrelated topics | 45 | 56 | 65 |
| Learning math is mostly memorizing | 44 | 64 | 56 |
| Math is sometimes boring | 49 | 46 | 46 |
| Math is boring | 21 | 14 | 14 |

Approximately half of all students believe that they will be working in an area that requires math when they are older. More than half of all students feel that they will need to use math to get along well in everyday life, and many more Black and Hispanic students than White students feel that it is important to know mathematics such as algebra and geometry to get a good job. Also, a large majority of Black, Hispanic, and White students report that they are willing to work hard in mathematics.

However, less than half of all Black, Hispanic, and White students say that they would like to take more math, and slightly more than a third of Hispanic students, somewhat fewer than a third of White students, and somewhat less than a quarter of Black students actively dislike mathematics. In addition, more than a third of all students not only find math difficult but also claim that they are either undecided, or quite certain, that they do not like to be challenged when they are given a difficult math problem.

Interestingly, more than half of all minority eleventh-graders report that they get great encouragement to take math courses from their parents. Also, more than a third of all minority students say they get regular help with their math homework from their parents. More than half of all students say they get regular help from their friends. However, roughly one-half of all students report that they spend either no time or less than one hour a week on math homework.

Most eleventh-graders claim that they understand what is being talked about in mathematics, but more than half of Hispanic and Black eleventh-graders are either uncertain or absolutely convinced that math is made up of unrelated topics.

Many eleventh-graders believe that learning mathematics is mostly memorizing. Not surprising perhaps, an alarming majority of all students find that math is at least sometimes boring. (An interesting side note concerning Asian students, but one that requires extreme caution in interpretation due to small sample size, is that Asian students who report that they are bored with math score the highest. The reverse is true for the other ethnic and racial groups).

## Conclusion

The data suggest the existence of conflict and contradiction between the attitudes and accomplishments of students relative to math. After reviewing student responses, one is left with a certain sense of the unreal. Reality and expectation, as displayed in the difference between the proficiency scores and some of the attitude responses, are not always coincident and, moreover, the affected parties seem to be blissfully unaware of this discrepancy. John Dossey, past president of the National Council of Teachers of Mathematics, Professor of Mathematics at Illinois State University, and coauthor of a National Assessment of Educational Progress publication on mathematics, described very well several challenges to American society in the area of mathematics education. His first challenge merits highlighting here as a conclusion because it seems to summarize the underpinning of the most basic task in enhancing all students' mathematical achievement.

In his commentary delivered at the National Press Club on the issuance of *The Mathematics Report Card,* Dossey (1988) suggests that

> the first thing . . . is the development of wide-spread understanding of
> the role mathematics plays in today's work place and in helping to fuel

our nation's economy. Data from the assessment and from other sources show that significant proportions of American citizens do not recognize this role. This problem is further compounded by the findings of international comparisons showing that Americans view mathematics as a subject where success is determined more by genetic factors (one's parents were good in mathematics) than by hard work and determination to succeed. Results from other countries show that their students consider success in mathematics an end product of diligent study and the application of one's abilities.

## References

Association of American Colleges. *Integrity in the College Curriculum: A Report to the Academic Community.* Washington, D.C.: Association of American Colleges, 1985.

Burke, J., Braden, J., Hansen, M., Lago, J., and Tepping, B. *National Assessment of Educational Progress—17th Year Sampling and Weighing Procedures Final Report.* Prepared for the Educational Testing Service, Princeton, N.J. Rockville, Md.: Westat, 1987.

Dossey, J. A., Mullis, I.V.S., Lindquist, M. M., and Chambers, D. L. *The Mathematics Report Card: Are We Measuring Up? Trends and Achievement Based on the 1986 National Assessment.* Princeton, N.J.: Educational Testing Service, 1988.

Mullis, I.V.S., and Jenkins, L. B. *The Science Report Card: Elements of Risk and Recovery. Trends and Achievement Based on the 1986 National Assessment.* Princeton, N.J.: Educational Testing Service, 1988.

*Janet R. Johnson is director of administration for National Assessment of Educational Progress at the Educational Testing Service.*

# CONCLUSION

This book provides some examples of how assessment of minority-student backgrounds, performance and behaviors can be important contributions to college and university planning for the future. This book also contains research and ideas about some important sources of data as well as types of data needed to understand better the needs of minority college students in order for them to succeed.

In Chapter Seven, Janet R. Johnson's report of recent mathematics assessment results from the National Assessment of Educational Progress (NAEP) illustrates how the 1980s crisis in educating America's youth affects American economic development as well as higher education. The low performance of American youth of all races indicates that too many of today's youth are not being adequately prepared for the workforce of the twenty-first century nor for higher education. The performance of American youth on the science, reading, and writing components of the NAEP measurements are similar to their performance in mathematics, and Black and Latino youth perform well below their White counterparts. The implication for higher education is that remedial programs and other interventions will continue to be needed especially for minority youth to succeed in college.

But Johnson also illustrates that minority students are taking more math courses in high school, which suggests that improvements can be expected as long as the quality of their schools improves and their interest and level of effort also escalate. From an assessment and college-admissions and planning perspective, it is important for colleges and universities to assess the relationship between the course-taking patterns of students and their attitudes, behaviors, and performance on NAEP measurements in order to indicate progress and to identify the types of interventions that are needed.

Outside of academic performance, the NAEP is valuable for projecting the academic support needs of future generations of students. The NAEP data base includes data about the school and community characteristics of students. These types of data are useful for showing the environmental factors that need to be manipulated in order to improve student performance and outcomes. Such factors include the size and economic condition of a student's community, his or her national region, parental educational attainment, parental occupation and employment status, types of reading material at home, hours spent watching television, a student's attitudes about academic subjects, and his or her study habits. The relationships of these factors to performance are not only important for projecting how students will perform but can also be useful in advising students and planning intervention strategies.

The effects of parental encouragement and academic orientation as well as environmental factors on performance are most apparent in Asian students. In Chapter Three, Jean J. Endo showed that the general perception of high academic achievement among Asian Americans is largely caused by the high academic performance of Chinese, Japanese, and Korean students. In the case of these three groups, parents assure that their children devote time to their studies and encourage high performance in school as a means of high achievement in college and in careers after college. The emphasis and encouragement is not as great on verbal achievement among these three groups, and this is reflected by their relatively lower verbal performance on standardized tests.

The high performance of these three Asian sub-groups relative to other minorities tends to overshadow their affective status as well as the lower performance and achievement among other Asian sub-groups (that is, Filipinos, Pacific Islanders, Laotians, Cambodians, and Vietnamese). In terms of affect, Endo illustrates how assessments of Asian college students reveal their need for more social interaction with faculty and other students, cultural enrichment, and Asian role models to enhance their interaction with faculty. Endo also shows that assessments that stratify the Asian population into sub-groups reveal lower quality elementary and secondary schooling, less parental reinforcement of academic achievement, and lower academic performance among Asian groups other than Chinese, Japanese, and Koreans than in nonminorities. Assessments of these sub-groups will continue to be important as the population of Asian Americans continues to grow in the United States.

Among the most important recommendations presented by Endo is that college and university assessments should take into account the course-taking patterns, student attitudes, and their nonacademic experiences in college in order to focus on providing Asians with a well-rounded education. Endo points out that Asians tend to favor taking college courses in the areas of their strengths (science and math) and tend to neglect courses that would help to improve their verbal skills. College advisers could use such assessment results from surveys and transcript analyses to strengthen the academic and social development of Asian students.

The positive effects of high expectations and high standards toward increasing motivation and performance do not appertain to Asians alone. In Chapter Six, Roy E. McTarnaghan illustrated how increased use of assessment as graduation requirements from high school, increased college-admissions standards, and greater use of rising-junior examinations in the state of Florida has resulted in large numbers of students taking college-preparatory courses in high school and higher test scores on high school exams, as well as higher college admissions tests and higher retention rates in college for Black, Latino, and White students. Student attitudes toward school and their study habits improved as standards and expectations increased.

Despite the evidence that minority student performance increases just as majority students increase when higher standards are required of them, the gap between non-Asian minority and majority student performance causes concerns not only about the quality of schooling but also about the fairness of tests and assessment tools. In order to allay these concerns, the gaps between minority and majority student performance will have to be removed and alternative means of assessment will need to be identified. In Chapter Five, Mildred Garcia implores assessors to be cautious and creative in the assessment process. Assessments must have construct validity and reflect the type of curriculum that students experience. Methods other than the traditional multiple-choice questions, which generally show lower minority achievement, should be considered, and they must be free of ethnic bias. Garcia recommends further development and refinement of "performance tasks" as critical components of future assessments that are more appropriate for minorities than the traditional tests.

Whenever traditional standardized tests are used in the assessment process, non-Asian minority students, on average, perform below the level of their White and Asian counterparts. In Chapter Two, Diane J. Simon illustrated the severely negative impact that traditional tests can have on Black and Latino student admissions into college academic programs and their entry and mobility into the professions after receiving their baccalaureate degrees. Simon points out that the problem is particularly acute in the teaching profession.

A critical consideration in order for assessments to gain broad acceptance and credibility is to assure that they are used properly. Daryl G. Smith, in Chapter Four, notes the growing concern among educators that assessments may serve as a gate-keeping function to keep minority students out of institutions of higher education or to prevent them from progressing through the college curriculum, rather than to improve institutional and program quality. In other words, the student rather than the institution may be too often the focus of the assessment and also the target of explanations for their success and achievement in college. Smith identifies aspects about institutions that, in addition to student characteristics, should be the focus of assessment toward improving the quality of the college experience and performance of minority students. Such institutional factors as the following are important:

• How much the content of the curriculum reflects the ethnic diversity of the student body

- How well integrated minority students are into the academic and social life of the institution
- Students' perceptions and their feelings about whether their institution values diversity
- The quality of the campus climate as reflected by the attitudes, opinions, and behaviors of students, faculty, and administrators
- Whether policies, programs, and activities are scrutinized and adapted, if necessary, to enhance minority inclusion and eliminate their exclusion
- Whether methods of student assessment for admissions, placement, and retention are free of bias.

Just as standardized tests have an impact on entry into the professions, Jacqueline Looney points out in Chapter One that they also play an important, although inconsistent, role in the admissions processes of graduate and professional schools. Looney's survey of the deans of the nation's most prestigious graduate schools revealed that while a variety of assessment criteria are used by graduate schools in admitting students (for example, letters of recommendation, undergraduate grades, and students' personal statements about their reasons for attending graduate school), the Graduate Records Examination (GRE) score is believed to be the most important criterion for admission. She also points out that, unlike the typical undergraduate admissions process, the graduate admission process is decentralized and results in inconsistent use of criteria (for example, some departments give more credence to undergraduate grades than to GRE scores, while others give greater weight to personal statements). Looney's survey also reveals that, despite the interest of graduate institutions in increasing ethnic diversity, many do not ask applicants to indicate their ethnicity in the admissions process; also, preliminary screening decisions are very often made on the basis of GRE scores, which excludes an inordinate proportion of minority applicants. Looney argues for acceptance of a broader range of criteria to assure consideration to minority candidates in the areas of their strengths.

This book has illustrated how assessment can be used to assist minority students, how assessment can be used to screen out minority students, and how much more investigation of assessment is needed in order to understand its effects on minority students. Assessment as a tool for assisting minority students can be seen when tests, for example, are used not simply for making decisions about admissions, progress, or graduation, but also for designing curricula and interventions for helping students learn and acquire the knowledge and skills they need. Assessment tools are particularly useful for students and for faculty, administrators, and policy-makers when such tools include information about the backgrounds of students, their educational experiences, their interests and aspirations, their performance outcomes, and information about the institutional environment.

Although standardized tests are sometimes viewed as obstacles to minority-student progress and achievement, they can also be useful in identifying the academic supports students need for improving their performance and learning. Standardized tests are the most objective and powerful means of assessment. Until the quality of the elementary and secondary schools that minorities, as a group, attend becomes equal to that of their majority peers, and their level of effort in academic pursuits resembles that of their majority peers, their performance will continue to be relatively low. Tests are found to be very important for predicting student performance in college, advising students to take appropriate courses, and deciding their readiness to progress to the next higher class level or to receive a degree.

Michael T. Nettles
Editor

*Michael T. Nettles is vice-president for assessment at the University of Tennessee.*

# INDEX

Abe, J., 39, 40, 41, 42
*Action for Excellence*, 19
*Adams* v. *Richardson*, 30
Admissions criteria, 9-10, 14; decentralized, 7-8; impact on minorities, 10-12; student perceptions of, 15-16
Admissions process, student education in, 15
Admissions testing, for teacher education programs, 23
Admissions tests, and math, 81
Affirmative action, 11
Affirmative-action slots, 13
Allen, W. R., 2, 58
American College Test (ACT), performance of Asians on, 39
American College Testing Program report, 21
American College Testing Program's College Admission Test, 27
American College Testing Service, 59
American Council on Education, national report, 54
*American Education: Making It Work*, 19
Amir, Y., 63
Angelo, T., 55
Anrig, G. R., 27, 29, 30
Arbeiter, S., 2, 40
Arciniega, T., 56
Arizona Teacher Proficiency Examination (ATPE), comparative scores on, 30
Asian and Pacific Americans: and admissions criteria, 10; and assessment, 37-38; factors influencing performance of, 44-47; historical and social background of, 38-39; performance on assessment measures, 39-44
Assessment: effect on teacher-candidate pool, 20-21; and instrumentation, 55; of minority educational performance, 37-49; questions and implications for, 59-64; recommendations for assessing Asians, 47-49; as a tool to assist minorities, 102; using caution in, 101

Assessment measures, performance of Asians on, 44-47
Astin, A. W., 1, 2, 7, 56, 62
Attrition rates, comparative, 2

Baird, L. L., 16
Baizerman, M., 45
Baratz-Snowden, J., 27, 29
Basic skills, strengthening, 32
Beginning Teacher Assistance Program (BTAP), 28
Bennett, C., 56
Birnbaum, R., 63
Bittner, T., 42
Blacks: and admissions criteria, 10; campus environment for, 58; education degrees earned by, 21; failure rate on NTE, 28; female to male ratio, 1; math proficiency of, 86-87; perception of test importance by, 16
Blackwell, J., 60
Blake, E., 57
Bornholdt, L., 57-58
Braddock, F. H., II, 2
Brown, G. H., 56
Brown, W. S., 21
"Building a Multiracial, Multicultural University Community" (Stanford), 59
Burke, J., 90
Burrell, L. F., 56

Cabezas, A., 39, 49
California Basic Educational Skills Test (C-BEST), 27; comparative scores on, 30
Cardoza, J., 57
Carroll, C., 41
Carter, D. J., 7, 56
Chacon, M., 57, 58
Chambers, D. L., 85
Chan, S., 43, 45, 46, 47
Chandler, T. L., 7
Chinese Americans, immigration of, 38. *See also* Asian and Pacific Americans
Class rank, and Asians, 39-40
Cohen, E., 57, 58

# ORDERING INFORMATION

NEW DIRECTIONS FOR INSTITUTIONAL RESEARCH is a series of paperback books that provides planners and administrators in all types of academic institutions with guidelines in such areas as resource coordination, information analysis, program evaluation, and institutional management. Books in the series are published quarterly in Fall, Winter, Spring, and Summer and are available for purchase by subscription as well as by single copy.

SUBSCRIPTIONS for 1990 cost $42.00 for individuals (a savings of 20 percent over single-copy prices) and $56.00 for institutions, agencies, and libraries. Please do not send institutional checks for personal subscriptions. Standing orders are accepted.

SINGLE COPIES cost $12.95 when payment accompanies order. (California, New Jersey, New York, and Washington, D.C., residents please include appropriate sales tax.) Billed orders will be charged postage and handling.

DISCOUNTS FOR QUANTITY ORDERS are available. Please write to the address below for information.

ALL ORDERS must include either the name of an individual or an official purchase order number. Please submit your order as follows:
    *Subscriptions:* specify series and year subscription is to begin
    *Single copies:* include individual title code (such as IR1)

MAIL ALL ORDERS TO:
    Jossey-Bass Inc., Publishers
    350 Sansome Street
    San Francisco, California 94104

# FROM THE EDITOR

This issue of *New Directions for Institutional Research*
examines some of the most important assessment issues
related to minority access, achievement, performance, and
success in higher education, as seen by leading authorities
in the field. The key issues include precollegiate preparation for college, the unique challenges for Asian American
minorities, the effects of new outcomes-assessment policies
on minority student achievement, minority-student access
to graduate school, and needed institutional research and
organizational changes.